MW01040373

the

Lovecraft
Necronomicon
primer

About the Author

T. Allan Bilstad has been a Cthulhu Mythos enthusiast since first reading H. P. Lovecraft's *The Outsider and Others* collection as a youngster. This was unfortunate, because, possessing a morbidly dynamic imagination, the author afterward became easily frightened by the nocturnal beasties lurking under his shadow-wreathed bed. A quick scan with a decrepit flashlight beam under the bed was the minimum reassurance he required before bedtime, knowing that night-gaunts, ghouls, or any other unspeakable entities would retreat before the feeble incandescent glow, allowing him to burrow unscathed into the safety of the blankets.

Years later, as a sagacious and rationally minded adult, the author giggles quietly when reminiscing about those nocturnal fiends and how they terrified him in his youth as he writes to add his puzzle piece to the Cthulhu Mythos. However, he still carries a xenon flashlight just in case of unexplained noises under the bed . . .

the

Lovecraft Necronomicon primer

A Guide to the Cthulhu Mythos

T. ALLAN BILSTAD

Llewellyn Publications
Woodbury, Minnesota

First Edition
First Printing, 2009

Book design and format by Donna Burch
Cover design by Kevin R. Brown
Editing by Brett Fechheimer
Interior illustrations on pages 12, 42, 56, 62, 76, 84, 96, 110, 126, 144, 150, 164, 176, 194, 206, 214, 230, 242, 248 and portrait incorporated into front and back interior covers © Patrick McEvoy. All other interior illustrations by Kevin R. Brown.

Llewellyn is a registered trademark of Llewellyn Worldwide, Ltd.

Library of Congress Cataloging-in-Publication Data
Bilstad, T. Allan
  The Lovecraft necronomicon primer : a guide to the Cthulhu mythos / T. Allan Bilstad. —1st ed.
     p. cm.
  Includes bibliographical references.
  ISBN 978-0-7387-1379-3
  1. Lovecraft, H. P. (Howard Phillips), 1890–1937—Characters—Monsters—Handbooks, manuals, etc. 2. Monsters in literature—Handbooks, manuals, etc. 3. Cthulhu (Fictitious character)—Handbooks, manuals, etc. 4. Horror tales, American—History and criticism. I. Title. II. Title: Guide to the Cthulhu mythos.
  PS3523.O833Z562 2009
  813'.52—dc22
                                        2009017866
Llewellyn Worldwide does not participate in, endorse, or have any authority or responsibility concerning private business transactions between our authors and the public.
    All mail addressed to the author is forwarded but the publisher cannot, unless specifically instructed by the author, give out an address or phone number.
    Any Internet references contained in this work are current at publication time, but the publisher cannot guarantee that a specific location will continue to be maintained. Please refer to the publisher's website for links to authors' websites and other sources.

Llewellyn Publications
A Division of Llewellyn Worldwide, Ltd.
2143 Wooddale Drive, Dept. 978-0-7387-1379-3
Woodbury, Minnesota 55125-2989, U.S.A.
www.llewellyn.com

Printed in the United States of America

Contents

Dedicated to the late Dr. Woodrow Feanib,
who unwittingly discovered,
during his short-lived horror,
that ghouls *can* climb trees.

Introduction to the Primer

Hello. I thank you for your interest in the monsters, creatures, and gods found in the stories of H. P. Lovecraft. What you are gazing upon now is a primer, written with help of my editor, Dallas N. Labitt, to aid the interested but uninitiated into the horrific creations of H. P. Lovecraft.

When I say *horrific*, I mean that word to encompass the horror genre of Lovecraft's literary works, and not infer that his works are atrocious scrawlings and scribblings.

Who am I? I am but a simple narrator, a character if you will, humbly paying homage to the legacy of Lovecraft. My name is not important. My state of mind is, and so also is this primer. As you who embark upon the literary journey, boldly going forth across the uncharted seas of Lovecraft's worlds, I shall be your captain, navigator, cartographer, steward, and klaxon.

As I am an avid reader of fiction, specifically horror fiction, Lovecraft has been a part of my horizons for many decades. And as the years do pass, stealthily as a gug (which see in this primer), the admiration for Lovecraft grows, his fans now renewing and rekindling that flame of fear, adding and expanding upon Lovecraft's small collection of stories with their very own supplementations and inspirations. This lore of information and writings has been termed the *Cthulhu Mythos*, named so after the most famous of Lovecraft's creations, the dread god Cthulhu.

As we fans were once neophytes and novices in the ways of H. P. Lovecraft, most of us started along this journey with no guides or aids. Just our wits and our dog-eared paperbacks accompanied our travels and travails into the worlds opened up by Lovecraft. As a child, I sorely lacked a guide to the terrifying creatures that inhabit those well-worn pages, and spent many a night cowering in fear under my blankets, awaiting the return of the dawn and the sanity of daylight. For many things live in the dark, in our imaginations, and in Lovecraft's books: things that walk. Things that stalk.

Things that talk.

Things that talk back.

But I shall correct this want of enlightenment with this book, written as a preliminary guide for those who are not wizened in the ways of Lovecraft's monsters. This primer will act as your tour guide to the various denizens found in the literary creations of Lovecraft. You can safely experience and know these creatures without the dangers that have befallen other readers. This primer is much akin to the *Necronomicon*, a tome that lists and details the monsters of Lovecraft; but unlike the *Necronomicon*, this book *hopefully* will not cause you to seek the asylum of a sanitarium.

Excuse my tone if I am scaring or alarming you, kind reader. H. P. Lovecraft was a horror writer of the top magnitude, and, as such, you should be aware of the terrors that can await, hidden within the written word upon a paper page or electronic screen. I merely wish to inform, not alarm. I shall leave the disquieting exhortations for those of you who continue reading this, my collection of data, or those who dare to venture on and peruse some dreadful tale of Lovecraft. Er, I mean "causing dread and despair" when I refer to Lovecraft's stories as *dreadful*, not that the actual stories are poorly crafted or hastily written in such a way to inspire a loathing of the actual tale.

I must insist you continue to read.

Everything you shall be reading from here on out is true and accurate.

Well, mostly true.

My friend and editor, Dallas N. Labitt, in preparing my manuscript for publication, has merely graciously rearranged some of my original text to clarify several elements in the entries, and provided the usual spelling and uniformly stylistic composition assistance. However, I have taken liberties in expressing my own opinions about some of these creatures of the Mythos (over the objections of my editor), which I hope shall not be taken as gospel or have the semblance of axioms.

I am certifiably not insane.

This primer assumes that you have not read the tales of H. P. Lovecraft, nor are you familiar with his horror literary talents. (But I assume you have some sort of interest, as you are reading this book . . .) Worry not, novice reader, as I will not reveal any plots, nor endings, nor any other spoilers from his terrifying tales. It is far from my goal to in any way discard or distract from the words Lovecraft used in creating an atmosphere of supernatural awareness. In fact, I aim to lay some of my own red herrings, as to provoke the curiosity of you, the reader, so that while delving into a story you may remember my words from this primer. Nor do I aim to cover every creature Lovecraft has penned, nor do I choose to be complete in my narratives concerning the selected beasts or denizens. Some details are better left unsaid, as they are truly terrifying, and Lovecraft wrote most of his stories to instill a sense of dread, gloom, and fear into his audience using words better left unsaid.

As you will see, this primer gives background information and critical tips on how you, the reader, can avoid and (hope-fully) survive when encountering such creatures in Lovecraft's tales. Why do I say this? Well, as I previously stated, this primer is a collection of observations, notes, and facts col-lected by myself over the course of the years while ventur-ing forth into the worlds of Lovecraft and the monsters that thrive there. What I have discovered is that these creatures and monsters are very nightmarish and terrifying in their own right, for a variety of reasons.

I repeat, I am certifiably NOT insane. (More on this ac-count later.)

Hanging on the wall of the room that I call my library is a diploma I received in medieval metaphysical studies from an reputable university of higher education on the American east coast, from which I earned this degree as an undergraduate. This embossed sheet of parchment, coupled with my years of experience, qualifies me to write this book as an authority on the denizens of the dark, the basement of the haunted house, the wild lonely open wastes, and the black corridors of night-mares—on these hideous entities that live in the stories of the master of American horror, Howard Phillips Lovecraft.

Please excuse me if I have startled your sensibilities with my erratic monologue. It's just that when I think about the images that Lovecraft has conjured up in his stories, my mind goes away for a bit to another world—the Dreamlands, in fact. What is the Dreamlands? you may ask.

You may. Ask, that is. And I will tell you.

The Dreamlands is the realm created by Lovecraft, where many of his monsters and deities hold sway. I may refer to the Dreamlands in this text as a seemingly real, possible, world, but it is, in fact, a creation of Lovecraft.

Remember, I am certifiably NOT insane.

Lovecraft's tales revolve around the horror of a narrator seeing what was unknown or hidden for good reason. The Dreamlands are an example of this. If many people started to see werewolves or vampires every day, panic and outright pandemonium would ensue, as those beasts of mythology can only be the products of imagination, right? They couldn't possibly be real, right?

Right?

Such is the case with the Dreamlands. If people knew that when they dreamed, it was in a real place and that what happened there affected "real life," the waking world, do you think they would ever sleep again? Do you think the fear of that place would drive people to insanity in their desire to avoid it at all costs, even at the expense of their own mental health?

"Maybe," you might say.

But what happens when you read a good horror tale about, say, a vampire? Do you not get frightened by the antics of that "monster," physically so frightened that you dread the night and all its shadows, thinking that a vampire waits in them to drink your blood? Silly to think about, but that is what a good story can do: take you into another realm of reality, where you react and act in. Who among you, my dear readers, has not put yourself into the literary realm that a favorite author has created, becoming so much a part of the tale that you actually have a physical reaction to the mental image you have created in your head from the collection of words on the page? Is that not "real," your feelings and emotions for the literary work you have just read?

Or is it? After all, fiction is fiction, and although it can resemble reality, it is but a shadow of that reality. Horror stories, such as the ones Lovecraft created, are just that: shadows of things that appear in real life. The words on that piece or paper or electronically amplified on that computer screen are not monsters, nor could they do anything to you; they're just a collection of symbols representing sounds quantified and qualified to a particular culture. If you could not read a particular foreign language, would not a horror book printed in that language be unterrifying and unscary? But by reading that tale and understanding that language, allowing yourself the "suspension of disbelief" and having the writing skills of the author evoke and imitate the feeling of reality in your head, are you not creating a "real world," a reality that it is "just in your head"?

Or is it just in *your* head?

When someone is scared, you can usually see the reactions of that fear presented in their body language or even their spoken language. A typical response would be a shaking of the limbs, eyes alert and open, and mouth open, either screaming or about to scream, or even choking out the words "Oh, no! *Noooo!!!!*" The person's fear is real; their reaction is real.

But what if what they are reacting to is not real?

How many times have you been terrified by some unknown sound, one you could not identify but that has registered as something that would not be healthy or sane for you to see, much less comprehend? Think about the last time you heard a noise in a darkened room or when you where alone outside at night. Was your fear real? Justified? Unreal? Was it not a product of your overactive (or even active) imagination? But once you have identified that sound as being made by something benign, harmless, or even silly, didn't you laugh, releasing the tension built from the expected fear?

Reading horror stories is just like that scenario. You are not actually attacked by a werewolf; you let your imagination create the reality in your head from the collection of images on the page. Words are just that: images of sounds and nothing more. On a piece of paper or on a screen, letters are simply cultural representations of sounds produced by the limits of the human vocal cords. These "images" are pieced together using rules and commonly held cultural guidelines. But if you allow that fear to build in your head—the fear caused by stringing together those letters, stringing together those words, then piecing those words together into sentences, and following those sentences into making a story (a make-believe story, mind you!) to which you have a physical reaction to the simple stringing together of some seemingly random scribbles or electrons—you have just sampled the "insanity" of enjoying horror stories. You have been frightened by nothing more than your own imagination.

Is it not insane to be scared of something that does not exist at all?

And that is what makes Lovecraft a master of the American horror story: he can make you shake in fear if you let him. Lovecraft writes about the insanity and horror of comprehending the world as it might be, a world that if it existed would be so terrifying that one would be rendered clinically insane within a blink of an eye.

Now follow me as I guide you through this "imaginary" world of Lovecraft, as I introduce you to the "monsters" that he created.

Remember, the beasts in the primer are all imaginary. All the creatures detailed here are the figments of one man's active imagination, and that his imagination cannot harm you.

That's why I am certifiably not insane. Lovecraft's imagination cannot hurt me. His monsters cannot hurt me. They may have hurt my friends, those characters in Lovecraft's stories, but they cannot touch me.

Tee hee.

H. P. Lovecraft: The Father of American Horror

Howard Phillips Lovecraft (known to his fans and followers simply as "H. P. Lovecraft," or even more simply as "Lovecraft") was a relatively unknown author in his own lifetime; his reputation as a master of the American horror genre did not come until after his death. Born in Rhode Island on August 20, 1890, and dying there on March 15, 1937, Lovecraft's legacy is the collection of tales of horror and fantasy written during his short lifetime that continue to horrify and inspire present and future generations.

"I doubt that this author is so famous," you may say. But take this simple test. Assuming you have not read any of Lovecraft's stories, have you heard of any of the following names?

Cthulhu.

The *Necronomicon*.

Abdul Alhazred.

Miskatonic University.

Arkham.

All of these terms of monsters, place names, or items are the result of Lovecraft's imagination echoing upon the blank page in front of him.

Doubt his influence further? Take any of those terms above and do a web search. Google any of them. Count the number of hits.

Lovecraft's influence is keenly felt today.

Why is Lovecraft so important as a figure in the American literary field? Well, for starters, I would say that his works have stood the test of time. Since the 1920s, when his stories first appeared with relatively little renown and without a large-scale audience in various pulp magazines and other outlets of titillating horror periodicals, succeeding generations have favorably evaluated the writings of this reclusive author, now himself peacefully moldering in a damp grave-yard in Rhode Island, and have deemed them worthy of passing along to the next generation of readers and connoisseurs of American horror fiction.

Just how influential are his works? Well, in 1999 H. P. Lovecraft was added by Penguin Classics publishing to the hallowed literary canon of American literature, joining such authors as Poe, Steinbeck, and Melville. This elevation of his stature among American writers had twofold results: one (for weal), his legacy of work will be preserved and honored for decades to come; and two (for woe), scores of college students will be forced to examine, critique, dissect, and otherwise drain away joy from the reading of Lovecraft's tales, as with all the other classics of American literature. (It wasn't until after I graduated college and was able to read for pleasure that I found *Moby Dick* to be a fascinating character study and adventure book! It's much more enjoyable to read a classic at one's own leisure, savoring each page for its own value, than it is to be frantically poring over the text, analyzing themes and symbols just to regurgitate back onto an exam the extrapolated information.)

I urge you to read the works of Lovecraft as an enjoyable pastime, not as if you were cramming for a test.

According to this humble writer (myself), Edgar Allan Poe is now relegated to being the grandfather of American horror and the macabre, with Lovecraft as his legitimate heir. Lovecraft, nourished at the teat of Poe's gruesome literary milk, was raised as such, and having read Poe's works as a child, Lovecraft even included a reference to Poe's *The Narrative of Arthur Gordon Pym* in his novella *At the Mountains of Madness*. And like Poe, Lovecraft wrote poetry that encapsulated the beauty and grotesqueness of horror (although the subject of poetry will not be broached in this particular book).

Lovecraft's body of fiction can be classified into two arenas: one being horror, the other being weird fantasy (with some tales crossing said artificial borders at will). I can imagine someone who has never read anything by Lovecraft deciding to see for herself how "great" this horror writer is, and picking up a copy of Lovecraft's short story "The Cats of Ulthar." After reading the tale, this person might say, "Wow, that wasn't scary. In fact, it was weird and had a fantastic, almost fairy-tale quality to it." And this critique would be true, as "The Cats of Ulthar" is one of Lovecraft's more famous "weird fantasy" stories. (At the end of this primer, I recommend some of Lovecraft's better stories as examples of his works in both the horror and weird-fantasy arenas.)

How did Lovecraft come to craft such weird (but delightfully entertaining) fantasy and spine-tingling tales of terror and dread? Well, there were two main influences on Lovecraft's works: one was the literature that preceded him.

Another influence was his own life story.

I shall now move on to the less frightful influence: the authors that Lovecraft read and loved.

Literary Influences on Lovecraft's Work: The Horror

Lovecraft's horror writings are straightforward in approach, with the goal to scare, terrify, or despair the reader. But there is a bit more to his writings than just this terror. Consider this quotation:

"A certain atmosphere of breathless and unexplainable dread of outer, unknown forces must be present; and there must be a hint, expressed with a seriousness and portentousness becoming its subject, of that most terrible conception of the human brain—a malign and particular suspension or defeat of those fixed laws of Nature which are our only safeguard against the assaults of chaos and the dæmons of unplumbed space." This quotation is from Lovecraft's long essay (or book, depending on its format in print) "Supernatural Horror in Literature," which is recommended reading for anyone who wishes to learn more about what Lovecraft thought and believed about the role (and history) of horror writings. (I should also note that since Lovecraft was a staunch Anglophile, it goes without saying that his contributions only relate directly to Western culture—specifically, English-language literature.)

Edgar Allan Poe heavily influenced Lovecraft in this regard. If you like the works of Poe, you'll appreciate the works of Lovecraft, as Lovecraft took to heart the guidelines for a successful short story as laid out neatly by Poe. This is not to say that Lovecraft did not venture from said guidelines, nor does it imply that everything Lovecraft wrote was a pure gold idol, worthy of admiration and devotion. No! Lovecraft, as any mortal artist in the realm of letters, made his share of silver "second place" medals, brass trinkets, and lead sinkers. Because Lovecraft has been deemed so masterful of his craft, publishers have compiled all of his works for publication (and I do mean *all*, even his most puerile stories written when he was but a mere lad in his teens!). Some of these stories, especially those written when Lovecraft was quite young, are mere doodlings upon which he honed and practiced his talents at penning onto paper the monsters that terrify. Like Poe, Lovecraft, in addition to tales of the macabre, wrote detective fiction, science fiction, and pure fantasy, but with the underlying thread of dread and terror, since the horror writings of Lovecraft were also tempered by his love of the fantastic and "weird."

Now-famous short stories by several other authors also influenced the writings of Lovecraft. Listen, as you read Lovecraft, for echoes of Henry James' *The Turn of the Screw*, Charlotte Perkins Gilman's "The Yellow Wall Paper," or W. W. Jacobs' "The Monkey's Paw." (If you have not read any of these stories, I urge you to do so immediately, but especially at night when all is still and quiet . . .) Robert W. Chambers' book *The King in Yellow* also had an impact on Lovecraft, for Lovecraft referenced a play of the same name in some of his stories.

Literary Influences on Lovecraft's Work: The Weird

The "weird fantasy" comes from the influence of other writers, specifically Lord Dunsany, who wrote stories of fantasy that drew inspiration from such tales as *The Arabian Nights*, which Lovecraft also avidly read. (As a young lad, this book was in

Lovecraft's grandfather's library, and Lovecraft's work reflects some of the stylistics and fantastic elements in that collection of stories.) The fantasy elements are evident in Lovecraft's writings, as people fly to the moon and back, and names for geographical places are not found on any earthly map. Yet there is also a dark and ominous trend to these stories, which is termed "weird" (look up the dictionary definition of the word *weird* and you'll see what I mean). If you espy a title of one of Lovecraft's works, and you do not recognize the geographical name in the title, chances are you are looking at a weird-fantasy yarn.

Allow me to digress a bit and talk more about an important detail, whose threads are woven artfully in many of Lovecraft's stories. Indeed, Lovecraft wrote many tales concerning another realm called the Dreamlands.

This might be hard to understand, but bear with me. And remember I am certifiably not insane.

The Dreamlands are another world/realm/plane of existence, which mirrors our own Earth but is populated by monsters and human civilizations that have no counterpart on our planet. (In fact, the inhabitants of the Dreamlands refer to our Earth as the Waking World, and they welcome sojourns from the Waking World into their own, as dreamers have built the Dreamlands over the centuries. Don't ask me exactly how, but it seems the centuries of powerful terrestrial dreamers have added their own geography and peoples to the Dreamlands, but the Dreamlands also have their own history and destiny.) The peoples and landscapes of the Dreamlands have a distinctly medieval, Middle Eastern flavor to their technology and culture.

Travel by physical means and not by dreaming is also possible. The Dreamlands are connected physically by several unseen and remote junctions, which can be traversed by a dreamer dreaming or by someone physically traveling to them. Our oceans lap upon the distant shores of the Dreamlands at certain parts of our globe, and underground tunnels and caverns link to the Underworld of the Dreamlands.

Don't ask me how. If you have ever dreamed, you know that some things in dreams just confound the rational mind with their illogic. Take to heart the name *Dreamlands* if you ever dream about that place.

In dreams a person may travel to the Dreamlands, which is akin to what occultists call *astral projection*, but it is far different in scope and degree of realism. Whereas the person's intellect and emotions can leave their own body and take on the form of a ghostly body, in the Dreamlands a dreamer makes their own physical body, so the dreamer becomes a part of the Dreamlands, subject to its laws of gravity, vagaries of climate, and predations of monsters. Dreamers can arrive by their own volition, or they can attract denizens or gods of the Dreamlands, and then become invited (or forced) to range the unfathomable gulfs of time and space between the realms.

It is usually bad to attract the attention of the beings of the Dreamlands in Lovecraft's world.

People can die, dreaming in the Dreamlands.

Magic, curses, and hideous beings abound in the Dreamlands, much like a sword-and-sorcery story, and many an unwary dreamer has fallen prey to unseen perils or sly creatures who delight in the taste of human flesh—for somehow the meat of those reared on Earth tastes that much sweeter to the tongues of Dreamlanders. And not all those who crave earthly flesh are nonhumans . . .

Umm, I think it is best now that I return to my topic, the issue of Lovecraft's influences.

Another American author whose "weird" influences on Lovecraft are evident is Nathaniel Hawthorne, whose allegories and imageries are reflected in some of Lovecraft's better-recognized works. (More on what Lovecraft was allegorizing later.) Clark Ashton Smith was another author whose writing style and subject matter Lovecraft greatly admired. Yet another was . . .

I think this train of discussion is boring. I want to move on.

Putting the Horror and the Weird Together: A Short but Implied Biography of Lovecraft

Many other books or websites can give you a succinct biography of Lovecraft. I will only give you some basics, to help you understand Lovecraft's writing itself. I would encourage you to do a Google search for information about the life of Lovecraft if you wish, but you may also simply want to enjoy the works on their own merits. My years of college education have shown me that the life of a writer is usually mirrored in the life of his or her characters, and Lovecraft is a shining example of this. To understand his tales, one can look no further than his life.

Firstly, Lovecraft was a self-taught writer. He never graduated from high school; his vast knowledge of the English language came from reading books. (I warn you now that you should have a collegiate dictionary handy if you want to read his works, as the self-taught Lovecraft was heavily in favor of weaving archaic and obsolete words into his tales in order to help convey a weird and unearthly tone. But don't let that stop you, as Lovecraft was able to help his readers sense the meaning of a word within the context of a story.) Lovecraft read books voraciously. Being an only child, he didn't have to compete for the bathroom, food, or anything normally associated with having siblings, which allowed him free time to immerse himself in his books, uninterrupted. (Coming from a large family, I can tell you that a moment alone to enjoy a book was a rare and thoroughly exquisite occurrence!)

But do not let the "self-taught" aspect fool you, as Lovecraft was a highly intelligent child and adult, and he absorbed book knowledge as readily as most people absorb air. One of the main features of Lovecraft's writing style is his use of "fifty cent" words, words that carry more weight than the normal "nickel and dime" words we throw around every day, words that are esoteric and erudite. (Ha! Those last two are my fifty-cent words I managed to slip in.) But I think it was his upbringing and early family life that had the most influence on his writing style.

(Auto-) Biography of Lovecraft

In my college courses on literary criticism, I was taught that one way to dissect and critique the works of a particular author is to analyze the author's own life, and determine what, if any, autobiographical elements are evident in the text. Writers usually tell tales that incorporate events or experiences they have had in their own lives. There is no better guide to writing than one's own interpretations, emotions, and knowledge of facts and interactions with the physical world. Especially popular in American culture is the idea that childhood experiences and early development will be highly instrumental in shaping a person's outlook and perception of life.

Allow me to clarify the above paragraph.

Perhaps a person who was raised in a relatively stable home environment, who, say, lived in the same home all her life, will have a decidedly different worldview than someone who grew up traveling around the globe, living in differing countries and cultures. One would expect the stationary individual to develop personal values based on stability and interpersonal skills, maintaining and appreciating long-term friendships and family ties. The other person, the traveler, might appreciate the sheer joy of having new experiences and meeting new people constantly. Conversely, a person who had lived his whole life in the same dwelling or town might fantasize or dream about traveling, while the nomadic person might fantasize or dream about settling down, living in one area or building for decades. Life experiences can dictate life's expectations.

There are many therapeutic aspects to writing. One very important aspect is the release of inner urges or expressions, ones that can be released and coalesced into art forms. I myself enjoy writing as a way of expressing the fears and terrors that I have experienced by reading the works of Lovecraft. Hence, this primer was produced.

But imagine someone else—say, a little boy, an only child, whose father went mad when the little boy was only three years old and, five years later, died horribly, a victim of a disease that ate away his brain, leaving this little boy without a father figure, to be raised by a frail-nerved mother who, later in her life, also became insane, doddering and doting on her only child, becoming so highly overprotective that she even forbade her only son from going outside for fear of his becoming deathly ill. His smothering mother constantly told this same little boy that he was hideous and ugly, and that she wished she had a daughter, and she would occasionally dress her little son up as a girl so she could pretend her wish had come true. This boy was also raised by his aunts, who, being of a similar mindset to his mother, further compounded his emotional frailty. The only happiness the boy experienced was reading books from his grandfather's library—but even his grandfather, beloved as he was, was not to be around that long in the boy's life.

For most of his childhood, this boy escaped into fantasy books, history books, and any other kind of book that would cause his fertile imagination to break free of the stifling horror that surrounded his everyday life. This same child was also plagued by horrific nightmares, being visited by dark and disturbing denizens of the dreaming world. This boy, about to become a man and graduate from high school, suffers a severe nervous breakdown and never returns to school. At the same time, his grandfather dies, and the family's fortunes wane considerably, going from comfortably wealthy to destitute in a matter of years. His mother sickens and, years later, dies in an insane asylum, and the boy, now a man, has no career and no one in the world to call his friend, save for a few cats.

Now imagine what kind of fictional stories that person would weave in life as a writer.

If you haven't guessed by now, Lovecraft was that child. Themes of insanity run, nay, course through his works. In fact, one of the trademarks of Lovecraft's horror stories is that the narrator goes insane or is already mentally unstable because of what he has seen or experienced. (I say *he* because female protagonists are a distinct rarity in Lovecraft's works.) Since Lovecraft's own parents went insane, and he was raised by his strict and somewhat eccentric aunts, the threads of the puzzle that is the horror story are barely held together by the fleeting sanity or glimpses of understandings that accompany the self-made realizations and comprehension of the narrator. Usually told from the first-person point of view (the story is relayed directly from the character's direct viewpoint, and is not filtered through any other influence), the horror of the situation is increased, as the reader shares along with the narrator/character in uncovering, say, an occult tome written in the hand of a long-dead relative, or a creature that stalks the countryside in search of the narrator himself.

The narrator is usually alone in the world (much like Lovecraft felt), and feels the cold dread of an impersonal force bearing down upon him, with the power to utterly eradicate the narrator wordlessly and without remorse.

In other words, Lovecraft wrote horror because he felt horror every day. His stories are his life in allegorical form.

Lovecraft can identify with the monsters, as he felt he himself was one.

Of course, this is all hearsay and without any shred of evidence.

Maybe Lovecraft was just a gifted writer. Just that. Gifted.

Not influenced at all by his own life story.

Writing about Lovecraft, I want to express that I am not like any of Lovecraft's narrators/characters. I retain full control and measure of my own faculties. I may sound insane at times, but that doesn't mean I am insane.

Right?

RIGHT?!?

cthulhu m

A Brief Background of the
Cthulhu Mythos

Those of you who may have heard the term *Cthulhu Mythos* (also simply shortened to *Mythos*) prior to reading this book, I tip my hat to you. As Lovecraft's influence and inspiration grows, I would expect more people to have a germ of this knowledge, whether this term be read in print or overheard in passing conversation. This term has been in use for the past few decades among the fans and devotees of Lovecraft, and is slowly trickling out into the mainstream.

The Cthulhu Mythos, as I define it for purposes of this book (this definition has also been utilized by other authors in the genre with a very similar meaning and intent), is a moniker used to label any medium that owes its origin to Lovecraft's writings.

This term also applies to any medium that expands that same realm of lore. This book, for example, is considered part of the Mythos, as it is rooted in describing Lovecraft's monstrous creations, and helps to contribute and expand upon the understanding of and information about Lovecraft's fictional worlds. While Cthulhu himself may not be present in any of the stories, tales, movies, or other entertainment media, the name is recognizable as being Lovecraft's in origin. (Lovecraft himself once classified his literary creations with the terms *Yog-Sothothery*, playing on the word *sorcery* and on *Yog-Sothoth*, a fiendish deity described in this primer. *Cthulhu*, it seems, is more widely held as recognizable, but all these terms are a mouthful to pronounce . . .)

In addition to creating the Dreamlands, a whole world of fantasy and possibilities, Lovecraft also crafted a section of New England, populating the area with towns and people touched by aspects and beings of the Cthulhu Mythos. The most famous town Lovecraft created is Arkham, Massachusetts, said to be just north of Boston. Here, on the banks of the Miskatonic River, lies the famous institution of higher learning, Miskatonic University. Kept in the vaults of the college library is the dreaded and despised *Necronomicon*, penned by the mad poet/author

Abdul Alhazred. (Note the recurring theme of insanity.) Lying outside the city of Arkham are the village of Dunwich and the seaport city of Innsmouth. These two places are home to some of the most memorable monsters in Lovecraft's litany: the Dunwich Horror and the amphibious deep ones.

Lovecraft himself traded and collaborated on stories with his friends, colleagues, and peers, and this tradition has been carried on through the resulting decades. Because Lovecraft himself did not utilize a complete mythology, only creating a few select pieces of information to further advance the plot of his stories, the Mythos as a whole is (pardon my wordplay) full of holes. Hence, with so many gaps in the lore, writers have created their own additions to the Mythos, shining a proverbial light into the otherwise darkened corners of the Lovecraftian universe.

One of the most intriguing aspects of illuminating this additional cosmology is that this mode mirrors, in many cases, Lovecraft's own narrative structure: the narrator has bits and pieces of a larger puzzle, and only by learning to connect the pieces does the overall history emerge (often to the horror or doom of the narrator and reader).

The puzzle analogy is very accurate when describing the Mythos. Lovecraft began crafting the puzzle by working on a few well-tooled pieces—i.e., his stories. Other writers incorporated these pieces (stories) into their understanding of the overall puzzle (the Mythos as a whole). Just what this puzzle is supposed to look like is conjecture. Lovecraft's stories have a basic theme: monsters are here and some of them go away, but sometimes they come back with horrific results (usually when uninvited and no one else is around to help, which compounds the terror). Other writers have attempted to structure and codify the Mythos, arranging the Lovecraftian gods into opposing teams. Some of the teams serve on the side of humanity, while the rest would like to serve humanity as a side dish.

While Lovecraft originally thought of his creations as solely causing despair and madness, with humanity having very few allies, this tag-team philosophy only adds to the overall puzzle that is the Mythos. Since the puzzle is not defined, humans by nature attempt to define the indefinable simply to be able to fathom the mystery. Sometimes the successful comprehension becomes too much to bear, and then the idiom "ignorance is bliss" takes on a deeper level of meaning. Perhaps it would be better to understand the Mythos as a work in progress. More is being added; some is fact, some is theory, but the reader is left to cull and glean the scattered tidbits and determine for oneself what fits.

Have I mentioned that I am certifiably not insane?

While many readers of Lovecraft and the related Mythos contributors form a unified and rational structure to the puzzle of the Mythos itself, to others this may not be the case. Some lone readers may justify select puzzle pieces of the Mythos as being axiomatic, as the disparate pieces become a cohesive whole in the Mythos' order or structure, which is not readily apparent to most. Sometimes, this solitary person may see or even solve the puzzle of the ill-defined Mythos in such a manner that no one else can understand, and as a result write an idiosyncratic story that contributes to the Mythos. The majority of readers, while seemingly rational, may dismiss this "lone story" as being irrational, illogical, or even insane. Woe to that lone writer who is mocked for having a unique and seemingly contrary view of the Mythos, for that person may find himself fighting an uphill struggle to convince other readers of his own validity as a member of the Mythos culture. To those who attempt to solve the Mythos in their own unique manner, read this primer and remember that sanity is not the province of the majority. A solitary sane person can exist in a society teeming with the insane. And not all solutions have to be sane.

Let us now begin your journey into the realm of the Mythos. Next stop, the creatures of Lovecraft's creations.

cthulhu mythos

The Creatures of the Cthulhu Mythos

Hereafter lie selected creatures as described by Lovecraft. I have simply arranged the creatures in alphabetical order, for no other reason save a convention of the English language. There is no significance attached to the placement a listing in this schema.

As you look over the listings, you may have some reservations about how to pronounce some of these creatures' names. Lovecraft intentionally spelled some names with the purpose of creating damnably confusing pronunciation. So, to answer your unspoken question: yes, the names in this primer are spelled correctly. Lovecraft felt that by making the names unwholesome-sounding or torturous to speak in the

English language, the difficulty would add to the alienness of his creatures. (This "unspeakable" aspect of creature names is a trademark of the Cthulhu Mythos, so in the future anytime you find a tongue-torturing epithet that leaves you scratching your head in confusion about how exactly to say the name out loud, chances are the story is a part of the Mythos.)

I had toyed with giving each creature a metered rating of fear. The monster/beast/god that registers the most mortal terror in me would have been placed first, and then the list would have included creatures of decreasing terror. But what may render me petrified with horror may be palatable for another, and vice versa. So as not to impose my own criteria upon you, I have used the simple arrangement herein, where the first letter in the creature's name determines its order in the book. Please forgive me if you feel I have intruded upon your own sensibilities with such cataloging.

These creatures—some of which, such as the ghouls in the short story "Pickman's Model," are used at great length in Lovecraft's stories—have been cataloged previously in various other publications. The entries here are designed to give readers a rudimentary knowledge of the monsters without having to read the stories; any "spoilers" have been avoided to reassure the gentle reader who wants to maintain the mood and suspense inherent in Lovecraft's tales.

Physical descriptions, mannerisms, and other tidbits of detail are based upon Lovecraft's own works, with details extrapolated from the same readings. Whenever possible I have clarified with my own notes—these morsels of information being extrapolated from Lovecraftian sources. Normally, these sources are my own understanding of the literature, derived from reading between the lines, so to speak, but I will not tell what is written out in Lovecraft's stories and what I have deduced from my own interpretations.

I will leave that determination up to you.

Please note again that not all the creatures, denizens, or otherwise nonhuman entities created by Lovecraft are contained within these pages. Such a listing of all creatures would be exhaustive and, frankly, too terrifying to behold. For example, Lovecraft wove many tales about human sorcerers and the foul magic they wrought upon the world. A human who uses others of his own species as fodder for his own perverse and twisted designs, without any moral compunction or thoughts of regret: is that person still human, or is he a monster? Yet I based my criteria for inclusion on the nonhuman definition of *monster*; if the creature is human, then I would say nay to including them in this primer (with one exception).

But what about monsters that look like humans? No, Lovecraft did not write about vampires, or werewolves, or other traditional monsters of Western mythology, so there will be no such "mythological" creatures here. Lovecraft created his own ecology and environment of monsters, some of which have their basis in historical or cultural lore but have been embellished or expanded upon. Lovecraft thought the most terrifying creature was one you did not nor could not comprehend. Yes, a monster like a vampire can have a human face, but what makes that particular creature so horrifying is that the creature does not engage in normal human activities. A vampire has its own set of priorities and criteria, which are different from most "normal" humans. A vampire must drink human blood and avoid the light of day.

And thus it is with the monsters of Lovecraft. Most are easy to place in the category of monsters, for they are not human by any stretch of the word, but others have their own hideous and terrible machinations. Some monsters may attempt to pass themselves off as human, but that it not because they wish to cope and blend in, but because they wish to infiltrate and destroy from within.

As you read on, you will note that each of these creatures possesses some feature or desires that make them truly terrible to behold in the imagination.

Remember, they cannot hurt you.

Mostly.

Abdul Alhazred:
The Mad Poet

One of the most famous creatures of Lovecraft's stories is not a monster at all but an ordinary human being—specifically, a human male. (You will remember that I told you of one exception to the lack of human characters in this primer, and here he is!) There is nothing extraordinary about this man, as he has two arms, two legs, a head, and so forth—all the bodily characteristics that allow one to say, at first glance, "Yes, this is a human being and definitely not some sort of alien or unworldly being." However, it is not what this human *is*, but what he *did* that is out of the ordinary. No, it isn't that he wrote boring or insipid poetry (I think we have all been guilty of this at one time or another), nor is it the fact that he went mad (again, I think we all go crazy at least once). Abdul Alhazred made his mark in the world of Lovecraft because of what drove him to insanity, and the actions of this unbalanced writer continue to shock and dismay to this very day. (I am referring to Alhazred here, not myself as the unbalanced writer. Remember that I have a certificate stating I am not insane, something that Alhazred sorely lacked.)

A little here about Alhazred's life. He was born in Yemen during the late seventh or early eighth century CE, and traveled extensively in the known world, amassing lore and legends that one day he would collect and then put to pen sometime before 738 CE. As many stories of his life have been written by others contributing to the Mythos, I will not go any further into Alhazred's biography and background. What matters the most is what he created: an item so horrendous and shocking that, well, let's not get ahead of ourselves.

A writer and a poet, Alhazred lived during the refined and cultivated period of Middle Eastern history. While Europe was wallowing in the barbarism and enforced cultural ignorance of the Dark Ages, the Middle East was undergoing its own renaissance and flowering of intellectual knowledge. (It was this knowledge, utilized in the Arab world, that the Crusaders returned with back to Europe, which helped usher in Western civilization's own similar but later Renaissance.) Hence, the skills of writing and poetry were part of the norm where Alhazred lived in northern Africa, as opposed to the illiteracy and lack of education found in most of Europe at the same time.

As part of a culture with extensive knowledge of the classical ages and access to wisdom about the world unknown to Europeans, Alhazred grew up in an atmosphere where geometry and algebra were taught alongside magical incantations and alchemy. Alhazred traveled extensively; as a result of his far-reaching explorations, he drank deeply from the cup of occult knowledge, and such was the extent of his imbibing that his actions would only drive a normal person to madness or beyond.

Remember, Alhazred started life as a normal person. And he was fortunate to have been born in the enlightened country of Yemen (as opposed to being born in some backward country at the time, like England). Since he was from the Middle East, it is assumed that Alhazred was an Arab by birth. But even if he wasn't an Arab, he still would have been labeled as "the Mad," for the knowledge he wrote down was not meant for the ordinary person.

What Alhazred is most noted (and reviled) for is his penning of the dread tome the *Necronomicon*. In it, Alhazred collected the obscure, the suppressed, the forgotten, and the impossible, and put to paper information that was never meant to be read, information never meant to be understood or interpreted rationally. It is rumored that Alhazred was driven to insanity by the lore he had accumulated over the years of his travels, or it could have been the damnable sights he had seen, but even in his madness he wrote coherently enough so that others could understand what he knew. And this understanding was a death sentence, for reading the *Necronomicon*, even in part, can cause the mind to reel and recoil from the horrors that one can only vaguely discern but that, wisely, most choose to ignore. Such lore concerns the state of the universe and how it is the plaything of mad gods at best; at worst, the universe is the unholy, unwashed sewer of evil. Abdul Alhazred wrote of the many creatures that exist in the world about which humans might not even dare to have nightmares. (In fact, in the *Necronomicon* even Alhazred denies the very existence of some of the monsters he writes about, as they are too terrible to comprehend! His madness was not absolute . . .)

Into the *Necronomicon* Alhazred poured, placed, and prodded the lore he had learned as a warning and guide to others. Whether Alhazred intended to alarm or to lure others is of some debate, as throughout the centuries cultural, religious, and intellectual leaders have banned the *Necronomicon* as blasphemous, unwholesome, or unsafe (mostly all three at once). The Catholic Church in the Middle Ages burned any copies of the *Necronomicon* it could acquire, but at the same time, occult sages secretly translated the original Arabic text into Latin and Greek because of the wealth of information that had been collected. During the Middle Ages, when much scientific knowledge about geometry, astronomy, and medicine flowed from the Arab world into the European, occult lore was just as eagerly welcomed as was knowledge about the sciences.

Such translations continued to vex church leaders, as the information, once written in a language confined to Africa and the Middle East, now spread into Europe, where the languages of the classical authors were still known. In the stories of Lovecraft, characters are driven mad by the words they read, for then they understand utterly the ramifications of the lore therein contained and find only despair; but those very same people, who oppose the fiendish designs of monsters, find in the pages of the *Necronomicon* some solace, the means to defeat or thwart such demons. Thus, the *Necronomicon* is a two-edged sword. One edge can raise such unimaginable terrors; the other can repel same horrors.

And as such, the name of Abdul Alhazred has been and will continue to be truly both a blessing and a curse: a blessing because he revealed what was hidden, and a curse because he revealed what was hidden.

Too much of what was hidden.

The cause of Abdul Alhazred's death is not a mystery. He was murdered in a public marketplace in Damascus sometime around the year 738; the uncouth nature of his demise was reported by many people who, horribly, watched helplessly. Why he was killed is unknown, but eyewitness accounts are all in accord: Alhazred was devoured, *alive*, by invisible demons, which set upon him in broad daylight in sight of many people. (There are some divergent accounts of the Mad Arab's death that I shall not pursue, as the account I give here is the most widely held depiction of Alhazred's death.) This sight caused great horror to the those eyewitnesses, and most agreed it was holy, divine retribution for his meddling into the affairs of dark gods and foul creatures, his penning of the *Necronomicon*—a book that should never have been written in the first place.

While I tend to agree with this latter consensus, I have a point I would like to add. Let's say you are a creature, a most evil and foul monster, one whose very existence is unknown to mortal men. It is the Middle Ages, before the era of modern communications like television, the Internet, or even mass-produced books. You can move freely and easily among the huddled masses, going about your unholy desires, as there are none to stop you—for how can humans stop a monster that no one knows about? Let's consider this example and explore it in more depth. Let's say, simply for the sake of argument, that someone scribes a book. It doesn't have to be a book; it could be a tome, or maybe even a innocent-looking primer, but it is this book that details your origins, your strengths, your weaknesses, and, most of all, insists on the fact that you do exist and are not a dream of some poor demented soul.

Now, human beings, your favorite prey, read this book and take notice of your actions. More humans are alerted and tell others because of the shared information in this book. They arm themselves, take precautions, learn your strengths, and more importantly, your weaknesses and vulnerabilities. Humans no longer live *in ignorance* but *in knowledge* of you. You no longer have the freedom to move at will, to hunt and kill at your leisure.

How can you, as a demonic bloodthirsty beast, continue your long-accustomed and long-uninterrupted schemes before some upstart humans decide they will hunt *you* instead?

Hmm? What would you do? What *can* you do?

There is one thing. Perhaps, just perhaps, you can destroy the messenger, the one who has made your existence known. After all, if it weren't for this messenger, the message would never have gotten out. And with the messenger dead, no more messages can be sent . . .

I think that is the pretext for why Alhazred was killed: the very monsters he wrote about did not want humanity to know about their existence. I think these creatures were very clever in the way they did it. These murderers did not reveal themselves, only what they were capable of doing. And isn't that the most terrifying part: knowing not what they were, but only what they did? These monsters, while invisible, devoured alive a grown human male in daylight, in plain sight, in a crowded city marketplace.

And that's why I may sound a little paranoid (notice I did not say *mad*!) as I write this primer, because, like Alhazred, I have composed particulars about unseen monsters that may take exception to my words. I think the monsters are out to get me, but I laugh and tell myself out loud, "There are no such things as monsters, and certainly there are no such things as Cthulhu, or ghouls, or shoggoths, or any other such beasts in this book." I repeat this sentence out loud, over and over again, until I feel better.

Now I must get back to my writing.

Alhazred is quoted many times throughout Lovecraft's works, and it is Alhazred's poetry that is hideously pregnant with occult consciousness. Translated from the original Arabic, one of Alhazred's more famous lines is a couplet, which tells much about the dread god . . .

Wait, did I just hear some mocking snickering outside my window? I guess not, as there are no living creatures outside. I know this, because of what abuts the edge of my house. But perhaps you are the one in peril. Aren't you the one reading my words? Aren't you the one learning about these monsters?

I urge you to go ahead and say what I would say out loud in a situation like this: "There are no such things as monsters, and certainly there are no such things as Cthulhu, or ghouls, or shoggoths, or any other such beasts in this book." Repeat these words until you feel better, then stop and carefully listen.

Now, did *you* hear something?

Azathoth: Idiot Flutist or Idiot Genius?

According to Lovecraft, at the center of the universe there is a god. This deity, seemingly at the most important place in all of existence, would at first appear to be its *raison d'être*: the universe's materialization from thought into reality.

Now imagine a corpulent mass of swirling, chaotic forms and shapes, eerily piping a thin-reeded tune without any melody or rhythm. Around this deity, like a sultan on his throne, are similar beings, lesser in stature but of equal unquiet form and animated matter, each adding to the unwholesome songs with their own twisted and spiny pipes.

This is Azathoth, the insane and formless god, the mad mass of chaos who pipes his unearthly piping, from his beginning until his end.

The reason Azathoth and his courts play their pipes at the center of the universe is unknown, nor is it known for what cause they strive, as everything that comes from Azathoth is seemingly without order or structure. Such is the nature of primordial chaos.

Perhaps Lovecraft made Azathoth a metaphor for the whole universe—that the universe exists because of chaos, and with chaos it still creates. In his stories, Lovecraft mentions that human sorcerers sometimes appeal to this insane god with supplications and rituals to curry his favor. These sorcerers, robed in astrological and mystical, symbol-laden imageries, form a society, a priesthood if you will, that attempts to make sense of the senseless. These followers hope their prayers will fall upon sympathetic ears: ears in the center of the universe, ears that can only hear the sounds of their own tunes created on unholy and foul pipes.

Do you see what a man could think if he felt that the world was only the cause of insanity and chaos? Lovecraft did, and this axiom he expressed so carefully and calculatingly in his stories of entertainment.

Azathoth, as with many literary creations, is a symbol of a larger whole, a puzzle piece of a puzzle, but perhaps the puzzle has no solutions or meaning.

One would not know if the puzzle does have meaning until one starts to piece it together. And even then, there may be only chaos in the structure.

And insanity.

Insanity makes the world go around . . . and around . . . and around . . .

Corpse Steeds:
Decomposing Night-mares

Corpse steeds are flying animals, and, for the most part, are indescribable because they come from a different realm than Earth. (This "indescribable" aspect is intentional on the part of Lovecraft, as true horror is generated from deep within one's own self, and can be amplified from tidbits of the physical world around. What is truly more terrifying to you: the "monster" half glimpsed in the shadows, or the "monster" standing out in plain view? As a child, I knew that even beloved family pets could be terrifying monsters when seen in the treacherous gloom of early morning . . .)

Corpse steeds are tamed and owned by formerly dead humans. (Now can you see why the creatures are so named?)

These formerly dead humans, not being mindless zombies but having full retention of their mental faculties, can be described best as undead wizards; however, any creatures with an affinity for corpses will utilize these mounts for travel. (Think about what I just said in that last sentence . . .) Since corpse steeds allow themselves to be ridden by the foul undead, one can imagine the imagery that bespeaks a description of such an animal.

Perhaps the best way to physically describe a corpse steed is to draw comparisons to known animals. The following animals have elements of the appearance of a corpse steed:

1. crows (wings and movement during flight)
2. moles (bodies and heads)
3. buzzards (elongated and featherless neck, their overall appearance when viewed from afar)
4. ants (torso body with six sets of legs)
5. vampire bats (composition of wings and elongated fangs with a wrinkly mass of flesh for a nose)
6. rotting human corpse (all-over impression . . . ugh!)

All of these attributes have been used to describe a corpse steed.

Ugh. Again, ugh!

And to complicate matters further, corpse steeds not only gallop like their terrestrial horse counterparts, but they can also fly into the ether and travel between realms. It has been reported that corpse steeds can take their riders into outer space to visit other planets, and also travel to other realms of existence, such as the Dreamlands, another world that is linked to our Earth but contains many magical creatures and enchantments. (More on the Dreamlands in other entries.) The corpse steed will gallop as if on the ground, and given the correct urgings from the rider, the steed can shift and enter the invisible ether that connects together the myriad realms of existence.

Such a ride is not recommended for the faint of heart, nor for the fragile of mindset.

No one knows how a corpse steed derives its sustenance; but from its decaying aspect and flopping walk, one could assume that the need to feed is unknown to these creatures. Although I would not put it past them to derive some sort of unholy nourishment: perhaps the corpse steeds feed on dead things, such as carrion or corpses.

Corpse steeds, while grotesque and nauseating in appearance, have the same intelligence as the terrestrial horse, and for the most part can be taught certain behaviors.

As such, I believe corpse steeds are, for the most part, tamed animals that would pose no serious threat to any traveler. However, if one does encounter such a steed, remember that these beasts of burden are usually in thrall to an undead wizard (or worse). Such an encounter with any corpse steeds would be best avoided for that reason. Undead wizards are very nasty and unsavory folk, and definitely would regard any human as nothing more than a trifle at best, a meal at worst.

And going for a ride on a corpse steed should be discouraged, as sometimes their crafty owners will use the steeds to kidnap the unwary. A cocksure traveler might think that an unguarded corpse steed would be the ticket to escape the clutches of a pursuing wizard, but such a wizard may have laid the particular corpse steed in his fugitive's path, with the animal trained to ignore all commands from the rider and return straight to the wizard's lair.

But no matter what I say, or what you may perceive as the wisest course of action, it still may be possible for someone to find himself astride the back of a corpse steed. The best advice to escape from a corpse steed while riding is to get off as soon as possible. Yes, you may hurt yourself in the fall, but plan accordingly (fall into a body of water or other soft material to break your fall without breaking your body). Waking up with a broken arm or leg would be better than waking up in a grisly dimension as a slave to an undead wizard!

Cthulhu: The Big C

Note: The name Cthulhu *has been pronounced differently by different people. Remember, the great god Cthulhu is alien, so if his name does not roll off the tongue easily, or you have a hard time uttering his name without stumbling, so be it. Lovecraft made sure his name was difficult in order to emphasize his otherworldliness. Think about it. If someone said, "Oooo, I have a scary monster to describe to you. His name is Bobb," chances are you won't be spooked in the least.*

I have heard Cthulhu *pronounced with the first syllable as in the word* chthonic . . . *look it up if you've never heard that word before. (Lovecraft loved to throw obscure and archaic words into his stories, so some research now will help you later.) I have also heard this god's name pronounced with the "th" diphthong as in the word* thing. *Either way is fine, just as long you are not reading his name from the* Necronomicon *in a chapter that begins with the words "To Summon the God Cthulhu . . ."*

Cthulhu is the most famous creature of Lovecraft's, and this ancient deity has inspired scores of artists and imitators since he appeared in the short story "The Call of Cthulhu." If you have ever seen an image of a frightfully intimidating and utterly gigantic humanoid with large bat-like wings and an octopoid face, chances are you have seen a rendition of Cthulhu. Lovecraft did not leave out many details when he described the appearance of the dread god Cthulhu. He (I shall use the masculine pronoun to define Cthulhu, but being an alien god, I believe that he is above gender classifications) is truly gigantic, and once was seen as hundreds of feet tall. He resembles something that you would think lives deep in the ocean. Well, he actually does dwell somewhere in the Pacific Ocean . . . for now (but more later on this little factoid). Cthulhu's body is truly monstrous—in size, in proportions, and in overall shape.

I call Cthulhu "the Big C," as I grew weary, when I was researching him, of attempting to spell his name correctly every time in my journal. Also, Cthulhu has many brethren (see the "Little C" section in this book about his birth mates).

Size matters, and Cthulhu intimidates on sheer mass alone. Normally (hmm, ironic, using this adjective to describe this

64

abnormal abomination), his height can be measured in miles (for those using the metric system, that's kilometers!), and his wingspan can be measured in the same units. Whatever system one uses, these dimensions are why he has been called "monstrous!" But, according to several eyewitnesses (myself, fortunately, not being one them), Cthulhu can render himself larger or smaller at will, as he is from another galaxy/dimension and the laws of physics only semi-apply to him.

But while his overall size can change, Cthulhu is remarkably consistent in his appearance. His most outstanding feature is his face, which resembles an octopus; he has a mass of suckered tentacles ringing his mouth and the shape of his head does resemble the body of an octopus. He has two eyes, large and bulging, and ears on either side of his head. From his back sprout a set of wings, as scaly or leathery as his skin is overall. He doesn't have any fur or hair, just a slimy outer layer of reptilian/fish skin and scales. Lovecraft's oft-used adjective to describe Cthulhu is *elephantine*. There is nothing dainty or petite about Cthulhu's stature or features.

If anything, Cthulhu is a horrific amalgamation of the most repulsive aspects of a human, octopus, dragon, and fish. Think about this for a while. Conjure up in your head what this description may look to you. Then multiply that image a hundredfold on the "Oh no, I think that image is going to make me vomit" factor. His image can arouse madness and insanity just by looking at him. (A fellow Cthulhu researcher, viewing a sculpture of the Big C at an antique store, once said, "That's not a horror, that's a Cthulhu . . .")

As I said before, Cthulhu is not from this Earth or even Earth's star system, but hails from a distant galaxy, possibly even a different physical dimension of existence. Cthulhu now lies/stays/awaits in the Pacific in his submerged city named R'lyeh. There, with scores of his brethren, he rests in the city, trapped by the mere arrangement of the planetary alignments of the Milky Way. The *Necronomicon*, Lovecraft's book that tells all about the Mythos and more, sums up Cthulhu's status with this neat little couplet:

"That is not dead which can eternal lie,

And with strange aeons even death may die."

Let me explain what this oft-quoted passage entails for you, the reader.

According to the *Necronomicon*, it seems that the Big C and his kind flew through outer space and landed on Earth millions of years ago. They built immense cities, fit for their stature, and then fought with other alien beings for control of the land. Eventually, according to some occult sources, Cthulhu and his kind were rendered handicapped by certain astrological planetary alignments, which caused Earth's atmosphere to become poisonous and even deadly to their kind. After retreating into the last of their cities, R'lyeh, Cthulhu and the others lie in a sort of death-like slumber, waiting for a time when the stars are right and they can walk the Earth again. This may take millions of years to accomplish, but they are very patient creatures, and not completely helpless . . .

Being a god, Cthulhu is not easily laid to rest. Horribly, the Big C is able to send forth his thoughts and desires to certain humans of the Earth. Those with artistic temperaments or an especially fragile psychological makeup can be influenced subtly by Cthulhu. He maintains a human cult of those determined to hasten the day when Cthulhu can walk the Earth and lay claim to it once again. These human cult members believe they will be spared from the bloodbath when the dread Cthulhu purges the Earth of its surface dwellers.

Did I mention that Cthulhu doesn't much care for humans?

At certain times, the stars and planets are in such an arrangement that makes it possible for Cthulhu to stir and lash out with his mental powers with less difficulty. At these times, dreamers around the world can be stoked and brandished to perform the Big C's unholy agenda. Activities that the Big C provokes include outbursts of homicidal mania and other inhuman savagery committed upon fellow humans with no remorse or regard for consequences. Those with a more rigid mental makeup are driven to create and expound the image of Cthulhu, so as to spread his terror upon the landscape. (When I said before that you may have seen an image of Cthulhu and not realized what it was, this is the reason for the proliferation of the artwork: Cthulhu wants you to be afraid. Very afraid. Very, very afraid. And he has used his psychic influence to spread that terror by revealing himself to unwilling people in their dreams.)

Did I mention that Cthulhu does not like people? Let me clarify. He has uses for them, and will utilize certain ones for his evil devices, but in the end humans are parasites and vermin, to be cleansed when he and his kind rule again.

So, if you are asleep and start to dream of an underwater city that is impossible to describe because its architecture is maddening and does not follow geometry or anything close to human ideas of proportions, and an obscenely shaped image of a tentacle-faced giant with wings appears to you, my advice is simple: wake up! Resist the urge to grab that axe and swing it at your fellow human beings. Resist Cthulhu's call to maim and kill and torture. It is only Cthulhu that directs you to perform such horrors.

Let's say you have a friend, a former colleague from your college days. Let's call this person "Avery." Avery is a talented artist of watercolor landscapes with a highly strung artistic temperament, and as such, he has succumbed to Cthulhu's dream calls. For days he attempted to paint what he had seen in his dreams, which kept recurring nightly, and he grew increasingly frustrated by his inability to reproduce the horrific but compelling images he had dreamed about. No matter how sympathetic his friends and teachers were, no one could alleviate Avery's self-induced obsessions.

Now let's say, for the sake of this example, that Avery was found one morning by police at the foot of the tallest building in town, naked, attempting to paint a mural on the brick wall, armed with only a bucket, a pocketknife, and a paintbrush. He had repeatedly stabbed himself in the abdomen with the knife, and the resulting blood flow he used as pigment. His baffling last words, according to the official police log, were "Cat too Lou, Cat too Lou . . ."

Now Avery had been always a bit of a flake, as artists can tend to be, and many were not surprised by his suicide. But when I saw the image on the wall, of a gargantuan head with sprawling lines radiating from its mouth, I knew the truth.

No, wait, I said Avery was a made-up person.

That's right, this example never happened.

Never.

That's why I urge you to wake up from any horrid nightmares you might have. In fact, I urge you to sleep as little as possible. I know I do, and while my doctor has warned me of the health risks of sleep deprivation and excessive use of chemical stimulants, I feel more sane and alert than I ever have.

Enough to write a primer about my understanding of the monsters of the Mythos.

Cthulhu is not trapped, but only temporarily restrained in his city, which now lies deep underwater somewhere in the Pacific Ocean. When the stars are right, his city has in recent history risen to the surface, enabling his psychic dreams of hate and torture to be broadcast without encumbrance across the sleeping mass of humanity, causing an escalating effect of madness and murder around the globe. In fact, I believe that World War I, World War II, and the resulting Cold War, in which humanity was threatened with extinction by its own hand, were the result of the influence of Cthulhu upon the world.

Don't you dare think I am crazy for thinking this, for how else can you explain the machinations of certain people in our recent past who have created weapons of massive destruction and then actually justified their use? The first atomic bomb was dropped to save lives. The machine gun was meant to make armies obsolete. The chlorine gas canister, the tank, the airplane: all of these machines were supposed to render the First World War "the war to end all wars." Examine the rapid development of technologies in the past century: the machine gun, poison gas, tanks, long-range bombers, missiles, nuclear warheads, and all the rest. Is humanity being taught from some unseen source how to make and use such devices of horror? What about large-scale genocide, made much more "efficient" with such technology? Leaders whose self-professed role model stated quite clearly that we are supposed to love one another, not make war on our enemies, don't seem to have gotten the message. Read the news. Does it seem to you that the acronym of the ideological slogan "WWJD" has now become "WWCD"?

Yes, what *would* Cthulhu do . . .

Cthulhu's Spawn: The "Little" C

The spawn of Cthulhu—or as I like to call them, the Little C—are the brethren to Cthulhu, the difference being that their stature and powers are smaller when compared with the Big C. From Lovecraft's writing it is not clear if they are the actual offspring of Cthulhu, but the word *spawn* communicates to the reader the watery existence of their world (for now, that is, but when the stars are right, the spawn will no longer be confined to merely dwell under the waves!).

Oops, sorry about that little revelation. I'm sure it won't happen in my lifetime. I have been under some mental strain compiling this primer.

Dwelling in R'lyeh with their lord, the Cthulhu spawn are in thrall to the Big C, who rules them with an iron mind.

Forging psychic links with his brethren, Cthulhu awaits the day when the stars are aligned, R'lyeh will rise above the ocean waves, and the atmosphere will not be poisonous to him or his kind. Trapped/sealed/sleeping in compartments all around the city, the spawn slumber and dream as Cthulhu does, although the reach of their mental powers is not nearly as pronounced or as strong as Cthulhu's.

However, some of the spawn dare not dream openly about the hour when R'lyeh takes its rightful place again on the surface world, and they can wrest the yoke from the Big C and rule the surface world instead of him. Then they can feast and glut themselves upon the myriad corpses of the human infestation of the dry lands. The spawn know that their ancient foes no longer have sway over the Earth, that now only the human race infests the lands and seas, and the numbers of these hairless but intelligent apes have escalated over the passing millennia.

The spawn are patient, so very patient. One day they know they will no longer be slaves in their own city but masters of all the Earth instead. One day humans will be displaced at the top of the food chain.

That day can be hastened with some help from the very humans who plague them. Perhaps with the right mental nudging and brief flashes of alien-inspired technology, humans could replicate the atmospheric conditions needed for Cthulhu and his kind to walk the land without pain or injury.

Perhaps the humans could develop a technology to alter the very gasses of the air, displacing the hated oxygen with its kindred carbon dioxide. Perhaps the spawn could whisper into the ear of Cthulhu that if the humans would burn the fossil fuels that abound in the Earth's crust, then the skies would darken with clouds of sulfur rains, killing the trees that produce the despised oxygen. Perhaps if it was suggested to humans that an internal combustion engine would be the technology to elevate humanity from its dependence on gravity and physical labor, then maybe the humans would be all too willing to embrace the helping hand that would ultimately ensure their demise, as the spawn of Cthulhu await their turn as lords of the land again. This theory, that humanity is slowly slitting its own collective throat, makes sense as I read the newspaper and analyze how mankind is just now realizing the effects of global warming.

Do you think I am still insane? Or maybe I am the sane one, watching my world with the calculated logic of occult knowledge . . .

Dagon: God of the Deep?

There also dwells in the ocean's deep another god who is not of this Earth. Where he comes from, no scholar of the occult is certain, but one may suspect that this terror is allied with Cthulhu, as both of the monsters call the ocean floor their home. While this deity has his own nonhuman followers, he also has a cult of humans who pray for and beseech his aid.

This god's name is Dagon.

While Lovecraft did not wholly intend the Philistine fish-god to be the same divine being of biblical derivation, it is implied in the stories that the mythological Dagon was in part an incomplete understanding of the Mythos monster. The historical Dagon has been described or called a fish-man, with the upper body of a man and the lower body of a fish.

This understanding may be faulty due to the antipathy of biblical sources that catalog the historical Dagon's cultural worship; but even if flawed, this comprehension of this fish-man aids us in facilitating the knowledge of this selected deity.

A simple description of the body of this monstrous god is *fishlike humanoid*. His worshippers have elected to represent the Mythos Dagon as an enlarged deep one (see the next chapter on deep ones, creatures that also live on the ocean floor). Dagon has two arms and two legs—his limbs are in the relative shape of their human equivalents but with webbed hands and feet. His face is human in proportion, but with huge bulging eyes, flabby fish lips, and gills. As I said, Dagon has been described as a magnified deep one, but I need to describe what factor of magnification I'm bantering about here. Deep ones grow to human height and weight, so when I say enlarged, I mean . . . well, let me put his size into context.

Dagon feasts on whales. And I don't mean the immature calves or the smaller species of whales. I am talking about full-grown sperm whales, and even blue whales. These whales can plummet the deepest, darkest ocean depths. And when I say *feasts*, I don't mean "only eating part of a whale." I mean "a feast of the whole whale, bones and all." That's how big

Dagon is. Although he is only slighter smaller in size than a blue whale, it is his appetite that makes him much larger.

Have you heard about the marine biologists who have examined specific wounds or scars on blue whales that were caused by other creatures, and deduced from the size of the wounds and scars that living in the depths are some fauna, unknown to science, that are massive enough in size, gigantic enough to prey on the largest animal known to mankind? I think Lovecraft has a clue to what these creatures are . . .

Since you have read this primer's chapter on Cthulhu, you know that the Big C and his kind came to Earth from an unknown region of outer space, and now live beneath the waves in their cyclopean city, entombed but passively waiting for the day when they can walk the Earth again. It is some comfort that the dread god Cthulhu and his ilk cannot move across the face of the Earth at will, and only at certain times can they actually mentally and psychically influence human mortals, much less physically remove themselves from their city/cemetery. One would only hope that Dagon is confined to his city, as Cthulhu is in his city of R'lyeh. But what could make those massive wounds on blue whales, which dwell in the ocean's void yet come to the surface to happen across humans? What sort of hunger would drive one to attack and eat those massive beasts? And is that hunger slaked on whales alone?

The answer to the last question is a definite *no*.

Dagon can leave his watery home whenever he chooses.

Think now about those last two sentences and what they imply.

Relying on arcane magic and alien occult sciences, Dagon and his followers are more active in their engagement of humanity. While Dagon rules from an unknown location on the floor of the Pacific Ocean, his city, unlike Cthulhu's R'lyeh, can come to the surface whenever Dagon wishes it.

Whenever Dagon wishes it.

Whether Dagon learned the magic prior to coming to Earth or he learned the arcane lore later, it is not known, but Dagon can raise a section of the ocean floor, and bring to the light of day portions of his city. He does this through mighty magic involving stone monuments, colossal works of antediluvian masonry that are in scale to his stature. Dagon will chant and recite vocal commands, and if the situation arises, he can work for days to make it happen.

After all, Dagon has a big appetite, and it's not just for whales.

I said that Dagon has human worshippers. Cults of his worshippers are prevalent among ocean-facing communities, especially those whose economies are dependent upon the vagaries of fishing. If summoned through the proper channels (i.e., dedicated chanting or recitation of oral spells that will attract his attentions), Dagon, as a god of the sea, can herd or coerce select species of fish into the waiting nets of human fishermen. But how does this knowledge of summoning Dagon get transmitted to humans?

Usually, a deep one (commonly a human-looking one, but it can be a full-blooded deep one) approaches a lone human, such as a fisherman plying his trade. Such a person would be alone along the ocean shore, or in a boat away from shore. Usually, this person approached is in a state of despair, either due to hunger or some injury. In either case, the person is out of sight of other people. A deep one, sensing the emotional state of this solo human, approaches this person and makes an offer he cannot refuse: "Learn how to summon Dagon, and he can feed you and your people with untold numbers of fish, or else you can die. Now."

This tactic is very effective, as most who are approached do value their own lives and those of the people in their community.

Having learned the rudimentary spells for summoning Dagon vocally, this fisherman may set out nets or fishing lines, then try out the spell, and is usually very surprised by the abundant wealth of aquatic sea life that is corralled into waiting weirs or baited hooks. With added summoning, Dagon will send forth deep ones as contacts, who then drive bargains for the rare and highly crafted precious-metal jewelry that deep ones are famously (or infamously) known for. (Read the section on deep ones to find out what these aquatic humanoid monsters desire most when trading.)

So Dagon acquires a "benevolent" reputation among his human followers, and his worship is spread by word of mouth from community to community. Some people reject such teachings out of fear of "idol worship" or other beliefs, but the sight of Dagon is impressive enough to convert most nonbelievers to his side. In order to facilitate this conversion, the Esoteric Order of Dagon is an organized cult that strives to make the worship of Dagon the sole church in any community where his name is mentioned with praise or gratitude. And if any other churches or worship communities actively resist the domination of the Esoteric Order of Dagon, such people will find themselves, while they sleep, visited by hostile deep ones or murderous cult members. Such people are then taken to the presence of Dagon.

Can you hazard a guess as to what Dagon loves to snack on?

Dagon will impart small pieces of his arcane lore and knowledge to select humans, if he feels that they can further his influence among the nonbelieving and noncompliant. Such lore might include spells to summon fish, capsize boats, or even a deadly magic that alerts Dagon to the location of the target at all times. Such a spell, which is akin to implanting a tracking device in a person, makes it impossible for someone to hide from Dagon. And as long as there is a large body of water nearby, Dagon can search for this person and obtain them for . . . well, Dagon is not just the god of the deep, but also of appetites.

Deep Ones: They Fish for Men, and Women . . .

Deep ones is the moniker given to a race of amphibious human-oid creatures. The name derives from the preferred haven of these creatures—the deep ocean floor. These creatures can, however, dwell at ease on both dry land and in salt-water environments, forming large communities on the surface of the Earth and in even larger cities underwater.

The origins of the deep ones are obscure. It is said that the race came from the stars, as did Cthulhu and his kind. The *Necronomicon* holds many answers to the riddle of the deep ones' origins, but few who have read that tome are able to comprehend all that is written there about these fish-faced fishers of men and women.

There are two kinds of deep ones: the humanlike and the amphibian-like. Deep ones share the same basic genetic pool as humans. This may in part be due to the devices of the primordial gods who tampered with the evolution of humanity's simian ancestors in the remote past, or it may be a result of species interbreeding. (Now, I know the scientific minds in my audience may say, "It is well-nigh impossible for different species to interbreed!" But we are talking about monsters here. Monsters, by their very nature, can do the impossible . . .) There are few visual characteristics to determine if a human is a deep one; but once you see a amphibian deep one, you will have no doubt as to what it is.

Think of the deep ones as the evolutionary link between fish and humans, if humans had evolved from piranhas instead of monkeys . . .

The humanlike deep ones resemble ordinary humans, and can come in any variety of appearance that humans do (light skin, dark skin, straight hair, curly hair, and so on). Body hair may be present but is mostly nonexistent. Eye color will vary just as it does in humans, but the eye color in most humanlike deep ones will tend toward faint blue or watery gray. Deep ones can inhabit any area (and more) where humans are able to live, but will tend to congregate and reside near large bodies of saltwater. Deep within their genetics (pun intended) is the call that links their species to the sea, and this call is so strong that deep ones will generally feel compelled to live in places with nearby access to bodies of saltwater.

This call to the sea can be sudden or gradual, and can occur at any point in a humanlike deep one's existence. True deep ones are nearly immortal, not knowing the advances of old age or the onslaught of diseases, and any stage of the human life cycle is mostly irrelevant to this siren song of the sea. In fact, once a member of this humanlike breed receives the genetic impulse to return to the ocean to complete the metamorphosis, this individual will do what is necessary to gain access to the ocean or any large body of saltwater. This call is very similar to the genetic message that migratory birds feel when the autumnal sun approaches, or the prompt that salmon feel to swim upriver when it is time to propagate. Such is the genetic message of the deep ones. Some resist, most heed, but all must obey.

However, a humanlike deep one does retain some characteristics that help distinguish it from its human cousins. A doctor would initially think that a humanlike deep one may be afflicted with a thyroid problem, as one of the features of these monsters are the symptomatic bulging eyes of this glandular disorder, which could cause an observer to think of a "fish face."

But it is not a glandular disorder. It is a genetic disorder, one that seeks to right itself.

Deep ones that can pass for humans may have wrinkles or flaps of skin on the neck, which are the buds for gills. With their bulging, fish-like eyes, deep ones rarely ever blink, another telltale indicator that the deep one is not wholly human. There may be skin webbing between the fingers and toes, and the skin may be clammy, moist, or otherwise scaly to the touch. A faint but pervasive fish smell may be inherent, which has its origins in the deep ones' skin, not necessarily their sweat glands. All of these features may be present, or one of them may not be apparent at all. It is indeed a rare humanlike deep one that can pass itself off as wholly human; it is rare for them not to elicit some sort of remark from passersby.

Remember, we are talking about monsters here. Monsters can do the impossible, and they can terrify us when we simply don't know what they are. And these monsters are intelligent, with primordial urges of their own.

As I said, certain deep ones can more easily pass themselves off to the untrained eye as being wholly human. It is only with degraded individuals, ones whose genetic calls have been made manifest, that these telltale signs may be evident and provoke a sense of repulsion from most humans.

Now let's talk about what a true deep one really looks like.

Imagine, in your mind's eye, a humanoid body (two arms, two legs, torso, head, and neck). There is no gender assigned to this body, no apparent sex organs that help differentiate a male from a female, as there are in humanlike deep ones. This body, for all appearances, is sexless. Now imagine that body covered with fish scales. The scales can be the color of any of the hues of human skin, but most have a fishy, metallic glint. Where you might expect hair growing on a human, imagine short fins or spiky webbings. Long lines of gill slits embrace the neck and jaws. Translucent webbing extends the length of each digit on the hands and feet. Talons terminate at the end of each digit. Thin lips circle rows of serrated teeth, and the unblinking eyes bulge forth from the misshapen skull. Now add the pungent stench of rotting fish to that image. Mix in some features of frogs, and you have a deep one. These creatures can grow up to eight feet tall, but the majority are the same height as humans.

Imagine that creature all covered with scales. There is no way that a true deep one can be mistaken for a human. Even a wild-eyed, delusional drunk could readily see the nonhuman-ness of these creatures.

Deep ones are amphibians. They are at home on dry land, or in the sea, able to process oxygen with both their lungs or gills as needed. Some deep ones will resist the call to re-enter the watery womb, and struggle to retain their humanity. They will don bulky overcoats and broad-brimmed hats to shield their ugly visage from curious onlookers, but this disguise is transparent, as deep ones have a strong, fishy smell to their bodies. Dogs and cats will raise their hackles in fear at the scent of a deep one. Cats will always flee from the smell or sight of a deep one, and dogs will only behave themselves after years of conditioning to overcome their instinctual ha-tred of this nonhuman species. And even then, such dogs will turn on their amphibious owners, as there is something in the deep ones' psyche that repels animals and psychic humans. Humans with heightened psychic abilities may be nauseated in the presence of deep ones, as deep ones are so alien and so inhuman that their auras offend and betray them to such people.

Deep ones ally themselves with Dagon, the elder god residing in the sea, and this race shares many of same physical characteristics of this sea-creature monster. It has been said that Dagon looks like a deep one, only one that is titanic in proportion.

But deep ones have their own agenda, one that is similar to most humans.

Dwelling in cities deep beneath the waves, the amphibious creatures of the brine view humanity as a resource. Not for feeding, but for breeding. Just as humans have a biological urge to breed, so do deep ones. And like humans, deep ones will want to mate with humans, to breed with them, to produce more deep ones.

Deep ones will breed with humans. That is how most deep ones start their life cycle—as babies born to a human female, babies who grow up to be humanlike deep ones. Keep this in mind as you read more on this topic later . . .

Having at their disposal the wealth of centuries of humans' lost treasures and sunken ships, deep ones will gather such precious metals that will not dissolve in the saltwater of their home, and craft these metals into ornate and superlative works of art. These valuable "trinkets" are then used for trade with humans dwelling near the seashore. Using the humanlike deep ones as intermediaries, the ocean denizens' goal is to secure breeding rights with humans, so as to produce progeny.

Deep ones are almost immortal, not aging or becoming decrepit once they fully turn into an aquatic deep one and lose all trace of their human ancestry, but they can die. To replace the ones killed by undersea accidents or by predators such as sharks and squids, deep ones seek to share their seed with the humans they can so closely resemble. And the underwater wealth available to them is so fabulous, so plentiful, that the inherent greed of humanity assures that the deep ones will succeed in siring a new generation, be it a result of the union of a human female and a deep-one male, or a human male and a deep-one female.

Yes, you have read that last sentence correctly. Remember I said that most deep ones start their life cycle as babies born to female humans. The lure of the deep ones' gold is so strong, so powerful, that human males have taken female deep ones as their mates. Some have even taken such mates as wives, siring a large family, all in return for wealth beyond imagining.

With such wealth, the deep ones are never far from a willing supply of humans eager to share their lineage with them. And deep ones are never bashful or lie about their intentions to potential mates. Deep ones wish to create more deep ones, and one day outnumber the humans that infest the waters and lands. That is their goal, and that is what they tell their human breeding partners.

Now, let me ask you something. Who is more of a monster, the alien and amphibious deep ones who desire to breed with humans, or the humans who sell out their bodies and their species to these monsters for mere gold and silver?

Who do you think is truly inhuman here?

DWÏ

dunvich horr

Dunwich Horror: I Shall Speak No More . . .

Seriously, I will not talk about this creature. Just read the story.

It's called "The Dunwich Horror."

It gave me nightmares for weeks. I could not sleep. Every sound of footfalls in the house, every creeping shadow outside, spooked my nerves and shook my soul.

And that was just at night . . .

Don't say I didn't warn you.

Elder Things: Resilient Barrels of Inhuman Intellect

What if plant life had intelligence? And what if that plant life evolved to such a state that it traveled across space, raised civilizations, and created such technologies that its ultimate doom was by its own devices?

Doesn't this sound a lot like the possible fate of humanity? Hmm, I smell a parallel here . . .

Elder things are intelligent plants not from this world. Barrel-shaped in trunk, elder things have short, fan-like wings that run vertically in a pair along the trunk's sides. Supported by five legs, the trunk of an elder thing is topped with five eyes. Standing as tall as a full-grown human, the wingspan of an elder thing can be up to ten feet across when its wings are completely unfurled. These wings are used for flights in outer space, and have also been used to propel the creatures in Earth's atmosphere. Such a creature is not a mammal, nor a reptile, but rather an intelligent form of plant, the kind that can live and thrive in the most inhospitable locations and environments.

The elder things are a very hardy race, capable of surviving for centuries in the cold vacuum of space. Landing on Earth millennia ago, elder things were the intellectuals of their time, being skilled in the ways of genetic and mechanical engineering. One of their most infamous inventions was the shoggoths (see their entry). Rearing their colloidal basalt cities on the continent now known as Antarctica, elder things battled other intruding races for domination of the world, namely the mi-goes and the Cthulhu spawn. With the astrological alignment hindering the Cthulhu spawn, and their technological triumphs over the mi-goes, the elder things reigned peacefully for many centuries. During this time, the elder things continued dabbling in genetics, giving rise to the dinosaurs, to be used as beasts of burden before the shoggoths were more readily used, and they even experimented with the genes of certain primates, in attempts to create an intelligent servant.

As the elder things grew more advanced in the ways of science, they became more accustomed to having their genetic creations take care of the day-to-day operations of their city, even to the point of forgetting how to run their own creations. Elder things withdrew into a world of art and philosophy, as they became more removed from the physical world and delved deeper into the world of the intellect.

Eventually, the shoggoths were bred to become more intelligent in order to help with the maintenance of the city and its daily operation and power demands. Originally kept under control with simple telepathy, shoggoths developed their own minds and wills, so that the elder things became fearful of their servants. The arrogant intellectual actions of the elder things culminated in the sinful slavery of their innocent shoggoth wards.

Is there a moral lesson here? A metaphor, perhaps?

Perhaps you should read some more works by Nathaniel Hawthorne . . .

Felines: Man's Best Friend. No, Really, They Are!

I would hope that you know what I'm referring to. I am talking about the common household cat. *Felis catus* is its scientific name. Kitty, Mouser, or Couch Scratcher are the more common and more accurate names.

"Meow."

And contrary to what I have stated earlier about the focus of this primer, felines are *not* monsters. Felines can save you from the monsters. In fact, cats are heroes in some of Lovecraft's stories. I have them placed here so that you may have a bit better understanding of Lovecraft's world, and the place that the master of weird fantasy and unspeakable horrors had for cats, in his heart and in his stories.

Forgive me for misleading you, for including such an inconsequential and seemingly trivial subject matter here. But I think you might need a break from the regimen of monsters being tossed at you, and some sort of hope.

Cats are found wherever humans can comfortably live. (Felines can even live where humans can't live comfortably.) Cats, let me state the obvious, are mammals, quadrupeds, and have sharp claws and teeth. They come in a variety of colors and fur styles (or even furless styles!), and they possess distinct personalities (or distinct multiple personalities in the same cat!). One thing that all cats do possess is a heightened physical sense of sight, sound, and taste. They are adept at seeing movement in both daylight and in near-total darkness, detecting faint sounds such as the tread of a mouse across a carpet, and they can even taste through heavy breathing. (When agitated or hunting, cats will seemingly huff and puff, which is their means of gathering taste and scent from their target/quarry.)

In addition to having such heightened physical senses, cats can detect and track beings from other dimensions. Have you ever seen a feline stare at a distant corner of the house, with nothing apparently there? This might be the feline way of watching a being whose physical form is not like anything of this Earth, and whose presence can only be detected by psychic abilities or some sort of light wavelength imperceptible to human eyes but keenly visible to a cat's delicate but finely tuned eye organs. And that is not all . . .

According to Lovecraft, cats are highly intelligent and social animals, lending their support to select humans, and even organizing armies to thwart the advances of evil creatures (read his stories!). Can the same be said about dogs? Lovecraft thinks that cats are inherently better than dogs, and he felt that man's best friend is truly the feline.

Lovecraft also stated that cats can physically travel from Earth to the Dreamlands.

"The Dreamlands?" you might be asking now, "What are these Dreamlands, and why would cats want to go there?" Good question. Let me answer both parts for you.

First, the Dreamlands is a realm of existence that closely mirrors our own Earth in terms of climate and size, but that's where the similarities end. The Dreamlands, as the name implies, are where dreams are solidified—created, if you will, by dreamers on Earth. The Dreamlands are accessible by certain rare entryways in our realm of the Earth (which is called the Waking World by the inhabitants of the Dreamlands). Such ingresses include portions of the oceans that ebb and flow to the Dreamlands, underground passages or caverns that connect with caves or tunnels in the Dreamlands, or simple flight through the ether. The Dreamlands are the lands where dreams come to life.

Second, this is why cats travel to the Dreamlands. By the aforementioned means of physical flight through the ether that connects Earth (the Waking World) to the Dreamlands, most felines travel to the Dreamlands to frolic and play with others of their own kind, away from the cares and worries of their earthly homes. Centuries of cats dreaming about fat mice to chase after or cloud-free golden sunshine to bask in for hours on end have in essence created a cat paradise in the Dreamlands. Think of the Dreamlands as the cats' own personal Disneyland. They go there to take a break, to relax, to play in an environment that is both fun and appealing, an arena in which they have re-created all the fun and joy in their own lives on Earth.

As cats tend to spend most of their time sleeping, they are accomplished and expert dreamers. Ever watch a cat sleep? They can twitter, twitch, and murr, as if their mind is engaging in some activity elsewhere while their body remains curled up on the couch. Sometimes these movements may be a simple response to dreaming about, say, eating a favored treat or pouncing upon an unsuspecting mouse. Sometimes cats (or humans) can astrally project themselves into the Dreamlands, and there they can learn of the rich history of that dimension, meet its unique and unearthly denizens, and experience the terrors that await us all.

The Dreamlands are not for the timid or the frightened.

Sorry, I digress. I tend to do that a bit.

Cats can travel bodily to the Dreamlands and back if they wish. This may be due to the fact that cats are such avid dreamers that they can will their own bodies into entering the ether and traveling. But as any caretaker of cats can tell you, these cuddly felines tend to remain grounded in their own bodies, willing subjects to their bellies or kittenish nature of play and amusement. But how do the cats physically travel from our world to the dreaming one?

A few humans have actually seen this transit in action, and those who have agree on the same details. Cats' travel to the Dreamlands is accomplished whenever the moon is shining brightly. Tending to gather in out-of-the-way places so as to preserve the secrecy of their trips, cats that yearn to travel to the Dreamlands simply leap into the air and by some unknown means they are able to soar onward to the Moon and beyond. Felines by nature are graceful, and easily twist and sprawl into the air with seemingly little effort. (I think part of the reason why housecats watch birds so much is that the felines are gaining flying tips and techniques from their avian friends!) Some cats journey to the lit side of the Moon, there to scamper and romp in the lush green lawns and forests of the Moon (which itself is a part of the Dreamlands, in case you are wondering, and such feline landscapes are common wherever cats deign to physically travel).

Having been widely traveled, cats experience and learn a great deal about their adopted realms, and share that information with others of their own species. This information may concern the best place to find wild catnip in the Dreamlands, or the forests to avoid where monsters roam. In fact, cats know a great deal about the nature of the monsters of both the Dreamlands and the Earth, as they are nocturnal and can see into the dark, which conceals from you and me the truth behind the silently sliding shadow across a bedroom doorway, or the dry scratch of a "twig" on the windowsill when there is no nighttime breeze to stir the slumbering trees . . .

So, how is it that cats are *really* man's best friend? Let's say you are in your living room, reading a good Lovecraft story. It's nighttime. You are alone in your dwelling. Your cat sniffs the air, then its ears flatten in trepidation. Suddenly, it hisses, seemingly at thin air. You see nothing, but your cat acts as though it does.

Your cat is not imagining anything. Felines, due to their heightened senses, can see or sense something unnatural there with you in the room. And your cat probably knows what that unknown menace actually is. Unlike dogs, cats will know exactly what their limits are when confronting the unknown. Felines are willing to confront a meddlesome rodent, or the sway of a breeze-borne leaf across the floor, but when it comes to ghouls, cats know best to stay away. Some may think it is nobler and more intelligent that a dog would bravely attack the intruding ghoul, but who would more often win such a lopsided battle? A cat's motto is *He who runs away will live to fight another day*.

So, if you are a caretaker of a feline (you can never really own a cat), whenever your cat starts to act very scared, as if it detects something unusual and it is deathly afraid to investigate, then this is the time to grab the cat and get out of the house posthaste. After all, felines have been to more places, and seen more things, than you can only dream about . . .

Lovecraft loved cats, and this may be the only source of hope that he offers in his stories; that cats will hinder and survive the monsters' advances. In fact, Lovecraft wrote in letters to his human colleagues and acquaintances that he considered his cats the only true friends in the world, and Lovecraft's love of the noble pets kept him sane during the dark times of his life.

Too bad the human narrators in most Lovecraft Mythos stories never stay sane. They could have sorely used a cat to keep them company and free of insanity.

I wish I had a cat.

Ghasts: Leaping Loathsomeness, Batman!

Fortunately for us humans, ghasts are rarely, if ever, seen on Earth. Ghasts are generally found in the Dreamlands, and even then they are rare, as they only abide in the Vaults of Zin, a series of huge, connected underground caverns. Ghasts need to stay underground, away from lights, for two good reasons. The first, I think, is that ghasts in appearance are, well, ghastly. I think they find each other disgusting to look upon. Ghasts can be classified as humanoid, as they do possess the head, neck, trunk, arms, and legs of a human, but their legs are incredibly long (a full-grown ghast can stand about nine feet high) and their faces resemble a shriveled skull, with sunken eyes, lack of nose, and a flattened forehead.

But the real reason ghosts avoid light is that they sicken and die in any light that is stronger than a gloomy twilight. The Vaults of Zin have many sections that are eerily lit by phosphorescent plants, which give the illusion of natural lighting from the sun in an underground environment. Even in such twilight, ghosts are able to withstand only a few hours before having to retreat back into the gloom of the dark. Ghosts are relatively stupid and animalistic in temperament, but they will avoid any sort of strong light source, just to be on the safe side.

Ghosts are very similar to ghouls (see the next chapter) in both appearance and diet. Like ghouls, ghosts prefer to feed on the dead, particularly corpses that have rotted within a certain time frame. As if that wasn't ghastly enough, ghosts have leprous-appearing skin, covered with boils, discolorations, and scars. Again, I think this skin condition results from living in a world devoid of light. The eyes of ghosts will, in dull lighting, glow with a sickly jaundiced and bloodshot luminosity. (Up close, this telltale coloration of the ocular orbs differs from that of ghouls, whose eyes will glow/reflect ambient light with a reddish hue that lacks any yellowish tinges.) Viewed from a distance, ghosts could be mistaken as incredibly tall but elderly humans, as they walk with a pronounced stoop to their shoulders and possess a most slow, careful stride, as if they were carefully treading in fear of toppling over. A careful examination would show that they are not human, though, as they do not have feet like human feet, but instead have sharpened hooves, very similar to a ghoul's feet.

But ghasts are not ghouls. Where ghouls have their own language and can even speak human languages, ghasts rarely talk, and if they do, it is a series of noises that sound like coughs. Ghasts do not have the pronounced canine features to their face, as they still remain human in visage despite the lack of facial features we humans tend to regard as necessary to be seen as human, but they do have fangs, and their beady eyes glow luminous but vacant. Hair is almost nonexistent on their skin, and they do not wear clothing of any sort. (I think this is one reason they tend to stay in the dark, as a naked ghast is rather loathsome to look upon.)

As I said, their skin is almost hairless, and the color of moistened ashen gray or pale white, like a mushroom in coloration and texture. Some rare ghasts will have a mane of dense, graying fur on their shoulders and neck, which tends to dwindle down their spine. I believe this coloration (or lack thereof) derives from their constant lack of exposure to sunlight or light of any sort, similar to the examples of earthly animals and insects that dwell in caverns for their entire lives. Since ghasts tend to walk like elderly humans and have graying hair and skin, you might expect wrinkles. Instead, a ghast's body is disgustingly plump yet lean, with sores and mottled blemishes.

Ghasts have long, powerful legs, which are heavily muscled, and this is why they walk very slowly and carefully. When excited, ghasts will hop, much like a kangaroo, able to cover about ten feet in a single bounce. (I deduce that this is why they walk so carefully, as they live underground in caverns. An excitable ghast will probably receive a nasty blow to the head from jumping into a rock ceiling). This hopping has been developed into an ambush tactic, and it is the ghasts' calling card.

The "hop and hurt" tactic is used when ghasts are threatened from another species, or even by one another. (Did I mention that ghasts can be cannibalistic? Oh, I guess I didn't, now that I am looking back over my notes. Ghasts will eat others of their own kind if food is scarce, or if another unit of ghasts is intruding upon their territory.) Ghasts will band together to select a wide-open area, with plenty of overhead clearance but with surrounding cover that can conceal a crouching ghast (say, boulders or rock fissures or formations that a ghast can use as a covering). Here, the ghasts will leave most of their numbers in order to remain hidden. To conceal their smell/stench, ghasts will scatter rotting meat or any other pungent materials that mask their own odoriferous presence. (Ghasts have an unusually heightened sense of smell, which I think is beneficial to any creatures that live in or near total darkness.) The remaining ghasts, usually the fastest ones, will then lure their foes or prey to such an area, which I call the "ghastly killing floor."

In such a killing floor, an attack is swift and unexpected, as ghasts will initially attack without making a sound, and they will launch their hopping assaults from all sides, so as to render their prey off balance.

I personally witnessed such an attack while on an expedition to the Dreamlands. In a section of the Vaults of Zin that was vaguely lit with the phosphorescent fungi common to the region, my party was tracking a band of five gugs, which love to eat ghasts, that ventured into the Vaults of Zin for a snack of ghast meat.

We watched patiently and from a safe distance, as the gugs were intent on securing their favorite delicacy. When they sighted two ghasts who purposely hopped into their path and then quickly turned to flee, the gugs lumbered after them, their gigantic strides easily pacing the ghasts' frantic hopping. We followed, and then heard the din of the creatures fighting. Led onto a killing floor that was riddled with the bones and moldering flesh of previous gug incursions, the ambushing ghasts now leapt in onto the backs of the gugs, cutting the fiendish giants with their hooves.

When a gug turned to face its attacker, the ghast would leap away, and another would land behind the gug to press its own hooves into the gug's skin. Other ghasts would leap in from the sides, avoiding the gug's huge talons and maws, then quickly but savagely bite the gug's arms and leap away, out of reach of the maddened gug. Weakened from constant blood loss and unable to coordinate their own counterattack against the nimbly hopping ghasts, the gugs spun violently on the floor, lashing out with their fore and rearward claws, horrendous vertical-filed fangs snapping on empty air. Exhausted, falling to their knees, the gugs were then easy targets for the ghasts, who finally pounced on the gugs' heads, coming straight down on their craniums to split the bone wide open with their hooves. The ghasts coughed in excitement and glee when the last of the gugs fell dead. We turned away when the ghasts began to tear and rend the flesh from their fallen foes . . .

If for whatever reason you find yourself in the Vaults of Zin, my advice would be to stay to the walls of the caverns and to avoid any tall ceiling expanses. Don't be stingy with your lights. Mask any odors you may have, especially your own scent. Remember, human flesh is considered a delicacy in the Dreamlands, and ghasts hunt best by sense of smell.

Ghouls:
Rubbery Graveyard "Dogs"

Ghouls are humanoid creatures, roughly the same size as an adult human, with some noticeable differences in physiology. While ghouls share similarities to the habitat and diet of the Middle Eastern ghouls, the monsters of Lovecraft are far different in appearance. Lovecraft's ghouls have skin that is rubbery in appearance (with skin color ranging from pale white to a dark black), facial features that resemble a dog's (flattened nose, slobbery lips, elongated incisors), and feet with half-hooves instead of toes (ugh!). While similar in appearance to ghasts, ghouls are smarter than ghasts; they are very intelligent, in fact, and form their own social communities.

And, oh yeah, like the Middle Eastern ghouls of mythology, these beings prefer to eat corpses. Human corpses. The older, the better.

Unlike ghasts, ghouls can be found anywhere in the Dreamlands or on Earth, but they prefer to live in or near cemeteries, in grounds that can supply them with a stable of rotting human carcasses and plenty of opportunities for digging and hiding. Ghouls can burrow and claw their way through the earth, even frozen dirt, making tunnels as small as the width of your shoulders to passageways in which they can comfortably stand up and walk upright.

Ghouls will dig their way through a cemetery much like a mole, digging from food source to food source—that is, from grave to grave. Since ghouls prefer to eat human flesh that has decayed and withered for a long period of time, graveyards that are newer tend to have fewer ghouls than graveyards that have seen decades or even centuries of human burials. (Remember, we are talking about monsters here. Human sensibilities, such as a desire to eat fresh food, may not apply at all to an alien species.)

Ghouls will gather their soil-bound fruit from below, clawing their way into the casket from underneath the interred container. This is why older cemeteries have pockets, dips, or other depressions in the ground where one might expect a grave top to be. (Yes, I have heard that these hollows are caused naturally by the decay and collapse of the coffins as they rot in the ground, but I know the truth . . . also, it seems that the modern, Western practice of burying a casket with an enclosing concrete vault to prevent such unsightly cave-ins from a decaying coffin only assures ghouls a feast with a sturdy ceiling!)

Ghouls have their own physiology that sets them apart from *Homo sapiens*, but they are as intelligent as humans, having their own language. This ghoul language consists of mews and tittering, sounds such that a kitten or young cat might make, as well as guttural noises that sound as though they are composed only of consonants. Ghouls can also learn human languages, and can readily pick up on the various human languages when living in close proximity to such communities. And because they are intelligent and resemble dogs in features and pack activities, some unknowing humans who have seen these creatures have dismissed them as merely "escaped circus dogs," not wishing to think further why a dog would prefer to run and leap along on its hind feet, and make no sound like a dog at all.

Tending to organize themselves into packs in their territories, ghouls are social creatures with their own kind, and have on occasion struck up conversations with patient humans. (Don't ask me what type of person would have the nerve to sit down with a ghoul and have a chat, especially at mealtime!) Ghouls are not the type of monster that runs and hides when lone humans approach, especially if they can detect fear or hesitation in the human. Curious by nature, ghouls will, however, avoid large groups of people, but will not back down from a fight when defending their home.

Ghouls use rudimentary tools and weapons, generally fashioned from items found in their underground environments. That is to say, if it is buried in a graveyard, it will be used by the ghouls as a tool or as ornamentation. Hence, ghouls will make clubs out of femurs, whistles out of tibias, cups out of skulls, necklaces made from finger bones . . . I think you can see where this line of examples is going.

And those are just the non-decomposing body parts that the ghouls craft into tools.

Ghouls will only breed with their own kind and will give birth like mammals, but ghouls are also able to snatch human babies to raise as their own. Such human babies eventually evolve and physically become ghouls, which tends to raise many occult questions about how this happens. And it has been known for adult humans to become ghouls, too, devolving and mutating into that horrid species of carrion feeder. Since it is common knowledge that those practitioners of the blackest magics are able to converse with and, with help of the occult (spells, glamours, or incantations), utilize ghouls for their own fiendish purposes, it has been postulated that the ghouls are able to cast their own magic to turn the tables on their human masters. Humans can devolve (or re-evolve?) into ghouls, but it is not known if ghouls can devolve (or re-evolve?) into humans.

The best way to avoid ghouls is by not venturing into their known eating grounds—i.e., graveyards and other repositories of human remains. While ghouls generally avoid any conflict, they will attack living humans if they feel threatened or if they are hungry enough. Ghouls are also known to inhabit areas adjoining graveyards, as long as they can move unseen and unhindered (burrowing under fallow fields or parking lots, inhabiting warehouses or rarely used enclosures, and so forth). Their skills at digging up graves (not "digging up" as we use the term; rather, a digging "up from below," not "down from on top") and forming seemingly endless stretches of tunnels makes ridding graveyards of their presence a Herculean task.

Ghouls can burrow from Earth to the Dreamlands and vice versa, so any ghoul tunnel you might encounter has a chance of being the conduit for any type of monster who is able to fit into such a tunnel. And since ghouls are intelligent, they will use ready-made tunnels for their own passageways. Such already constructed tunnels can be sewers, subways, basements, and so on. Any such underground area built by humans and not readily used can be easily adapted as a ghoul footpath, or worse: a ghoul lair.

The next time you are underground, put your ear to the wall. If you can hear faint scrapings from the other side of the wall, as if something is tunneling through the earth with sharpened claws, something seeking decaying treasures lost in the ground, I suggest you get out of there right away and never, ever come back. Ghouls prefer older, decaying flesh, but are quite happy to secure meat that they can tuck away in some underworld lair for a later and rather pungent banquet.

In fact, ghouls have been known to silently leap into open windows at night, snap the necks of their prey with their powerful jaws, and carry off their freshly made meal to enjoy later.

That's why I don't sleep with the windows open anymore.

In fact, I really don't sleep very much.

My house borders a cemetery, a cemetery that seems to be plagued by particularly large moles, as the ground is in a constant state of methodical upheaval and churning, especially in the oddest spots, nearest the gravestones . . .

Gugs: Giant, Silent, but Deadly

Gugs are horrible. Horrible. I think this word was invented to describe the gugs.

Gugs are gigantic humanoids, but I use the word *humanoids* very liberally here, as gugs are not human at all. Gugs stand and walk on two legs, but that is the extent of the similarities gugs and humans share. Fortunately, gugs are not native to our Earth, but live in the Earth's Dreamlands, in caverns far below the surface, and they eat a lot. These underground atrocities of the Dreamlands are not vegetarians at all, but carnivores, and because of this dietary choice, the gugs as a collective species are primitive and regressive, their civilization declining because, well, let's not go there yet. Keep in mind that they love to eat, and they are strictly carnivores.

I want to impress on you their physical description, so that if you ever see one, you will immediately know what to do . . . and that is *run away!*

Gugs are gigantic, and can grow up to twenty feet tall, which doesn't detract from their nasty reputation. Imagine the childhood stories you may have heard about giants and ogres, who are cruel and nasty and like to munch upon maidens, peasants, or even knights. Gugs are like this. They love to munch. In fact, they live to munch. Munch, munch, munch. On human beings.

Gugs love humans. Any sort of humans they can catch, but they love raw humans best of all.

Did I mention they are horrible? Horrible to look at, horrible in mannerisms. I have seen gugs but twice in my life. And gugs do not talk back. In fact, they don't talk at all. They let their claws and mouth speak for themselves.

Excuse me, I shuddered so hard at the thought of gugs that I had to stop for a second. If I can work up the courage, I will tell you about gugs in detail, in, excuse my redundant wordplay, *horrible* detail.

Gugs, like I said, are gigantic humanoids, with pale skin and shaggy black fur on their forearms, calves, and shoulders. Did I mention that an adult gug can grow up to twenty feet tall? I think they can grow even bigger, but no one has lived to tell about seeing one so tall. Save for monstrous aspects, when viewed at a distance gugs resemble humans in frame and symmetry. (Viewing gugs is not recommended. However, if you do insist on viewing a gug, view them at a distance. The farther, the better!)

One of these monstrous aspects: while gugs and humans both have two upper arms, gugs have four forearms. The difference here is apparent below the elbow. Instead of one joint at the elbow, gugs have two joints, one each for a pair of symmetric forearms. Each forearm ends in a set a massive, clawed hands, which can span a yard across, from talon to outstretched talon. One set of hands is predominately used for items in the gugs' line of sight, but the extra pair of hands can reach behind the gug. Gugs grab their prey by these hands and bring said prey to their mouth, which is their second most distinguishing but disgusting feature. . . . umm, on second thought, I will wait. Instead, I am going to discuss the features of a gug's eye.

Gugs have two eyes (like humans), albeit the gug's eyes are huge (around a foot across) and are protected by thick eyebrows and a bony ridge. (Imagine a Neanderthal's eye ridge, only jutting out farther from the face.) Whereas a human's eyes are set in front of the skull, a gug's eyes are set on either side of their huge, misshapen skulls, allowing them to see in an arc forward and/or behind them when needed. (For this reason, it is hard to sneak up behind a gug . . .) The orbs are pale pinkish in color, not white like a healthy human's, with a proportionately minuscule black pupil.

If one is attempting to identify a gug and espies glowing eyes in the shadows, the size alone of the gug's eyeballs would be indicative of the species, but in the dark neither height nor distance is always apparent. Realistically though, a set of pink eyes reflecting at some twenty feet from the floor would be a clue . . .

And now, the mouth . . .

Okay, I have finally worked up enough courage here to now talk about the second unique feature on the gug's face. Gugs have a mouth, and as with the human mouth, food is passed through it. However, and this is the most crucial detail, instead of a mouth that runs vertically like a human's, a gug's mouth is aligned horizontally, and is impossibly long.

The gug's jaws are set on either side of its face. From the lower chin to the top of the head, the sideways mouth is set with jagged and sharp teeth bordered by thin but slobbery lips. (A Venus flytrap with eyes comes to mind when one first sees such a face.) With bulging and bone-browed eyes set on either side of the head and the mouth running vertically, gugs look like a Picasso painting come to life (and a most obscene life, I might add!). Gugs love human flesh, but will also eat their own kind for both supper and sport.

Fortunately, gugs are only found in the underworld of the Dreamlands, having been confined there by the ancient gods of that realm. Gugs live now in their cavernous city built of many towers, the tallest being the only exit to the upper world. This latter unnamed tower, which encapsulates an upward-winding, colossal spiral tower/staircase, dominates the entire panorama of the gug city, and is the key feature in identifying the gug city for any travelers who may be unfortunate enough to stumble across it. Even in the bioluminescent glow of mold in the gug caverns, this tower can be spotted.

The aboveground exit to this "towering" tower exists somewhere in an anonymous woods in the Dreamlands, and its exact location has been a guarded secret by those who dwell near it. This round and stone-lidded exit lies in the middle of ancient monolithic ruins hidden by trees, and these ruins were the city of the gugs prior to their banishment below the surface. The exit is magically cursed and sealed to the gugs, having been closed centuries ago by unknown gods who were so offended by the blasphemous songs, prayers, and particulars of the gugs' worship ceremonies that they decided the gugs should remain confined forever in their underground city. All the gugs were forced to descend into this tower, and when the last of the gugs saw the light of day no more, the gods plugged the staircase exit with a great stone and even greater magic. While no gug can venture up and out of their unnamed underground city due to the powerful magical curse put on the doorway, anyone from the surface can easily pass through this doorway. The actual doorway, it seems, is intended only to stop the uninitiated or unlucky.

Hence, for those uninitiated and unlucky enough to stumble across this stone door, this is truly can be a one-way entrance, for the following reason. Few, if ever, live to tell of their discovery, as the gugs closely watch this entrance for descending prey who wander into their tower—prey with the sweet taste of human flesh, prey that was forbidden them centuries ago.

Not much is known about what exactly the gugs did to deserve such a fate (the gods who banished the gugs are unknown in name but had dwelt on the surface), so it would seem that these gods wished to save their human followers from the unwholesomeness that is the gugs. Much of the lore surrounding gugs has been lost to the passage of time, and I suspect that scholars were quite willing for such lore to pass into obscurity unchallenged. One tidbit that has survived may in fact just be idle travelers' tales, but it is said the gugs worshiped (and still worship) Nyarlathotep (see said chapter) and other unsavory deities. But since none of the gugs' written records exist (they may never have existed at all), all we know for certain is that these beasts are brutal, cannibalistic, and bloodthirsty, and one can easily venture a guess with those clues as to why the gugs are so deservedly entrapped.

Gugs, as I said, are cannibalistic, and it seems to be in their nature to eat their own kind (and even kin!). The banished gugs now normally feed on ghasts or sometimes even ghouls, as ghouls and ghasts resemble and smell like each other (feeding on carrion tends to impart a distinct scent to the practitioner). Ghasts are considered tasty to the toothy giants, and a good substitute for human flesh, and gugs are known to gorge themselves into a coma-like slumber after a particularly large meal of captured ghasts. Gugs will raid the nearby Vaults of Zin, a series of caverns in the Dreamlands, where some entrances can be found near the city of the gugs. There in the Vaults of Zin the ghast community dwells in near-total darkness, a ready food supply for the perpetually hungry gugs. The ghasts will fight back ferociously, but it is the gugs who are usually victorious, and the gugs consider the succulent flavor of ghast marrow such a treat that they are willing to venture deep within the ghasts' caves for days at a time.

Gugs will hunt and kill without mercy. Especially for food they consider most appealing to palate and sport. And *sport* to gugs means "food that runs away."

But what the gugs find even tastier than ghasts are humans from the Dreamlands. Even tastier than humans from the Dreamlands are mortals from the Waking World. Gugs will seek out and locate anything that remotely smells of a human, so strong is their appetite for crimson human meat. And the scent of one human from the Waking World (our Earth) is much stronger and more alluring than a group of any Dreamlands humans.

Gugs will hunt and kill without mercy. That is the sport of gugs, to hunt and kill without mercy.

Let's say that you are traveler from Earth, and you venture to the Dreamlands, only to find yourself in an immense underground cavern that has a towered city, with one tower reaching all the way to the cavern's ceiling. If by chance you encounter a sleeping gug, examine the immediate area around the gug for signs of a meal. Usually, this will mean bones, bits of flesh, blood splashes, and so forth. If you do see such signs, chances are the gug is in a deep sleep, and if you are very quiet, and if the faint underworld air current is in your favor, you might be able to avoid the gug entirely.

Gugs are silent, vocally handicapped, "speech challenged" if you will. This lack of sounds—even grunts, utterances, and any other nonvocal communication—may be part of the curse laid upon the gugs by ancient gods unknown, who were incensed at the gugs' blasphemous prayers and songs raised to dark gods. To communicate with each other, gugs rely on eye contact and movement, coupled with specific mannerisms. As gugs are not known to be able to see in the dark (as cats do), an encounter in the dark with a gug may be to your benefit, as the gug would not be able to "speak" to any of its comrades and thus alert them to your presence. Remember there is some light in the city of the gugs from bioluminescent moss, so stay in the shadows to be safe. However, screams, gun-shots, or any other similar sounds would attract more gugs, as they will drop their tasks and seek out any humans they might come across.

I think I know why the gods on the surface banished the gugs below. As I mentioned, I have encountered gugs but twice in the Dreamlands. Once, when I was dreaming and entered the Dreamlands caverns, I was fortunate to come across (unbeknownst to them) a band of gugs who were stalking ghasts. Like the capable naturalist I thought myself to be, I nimbly followed, keeping my distance in the twilit caverns, observing and taking notes, adding to the feeble lore that we humans know about gugs, intending to later write about my knowledge. This chance encounter I left unharmed (most luckily, as I was able to move very quietly and the gugs were too entranced by tracking the ghasts to notice my scent), and I returned to the Waking World, but with many nightmares afterward.

The second time I encountered gugs was while exploring those crumbing megalithic stone circles in an ancient forest in the Dreamlands. I had somehow linked up with a trio of dreamers from Earth, as we discovered a strange, round, stone door set with an iron ring that opened easily into the earth. (In fact the ancient and moss-shrouded door opened far too easily, which put us all in a state of panic, as we thought this area to be totally deserted for eons. But our curiosity overcame our consternation, especially our desire to find buried treasure.) Following the titanic staircase that wound down deep into the bowels of the underground, we did not think too much of the fact the gargantuan stone steps were not made for the stature of humans, but for some being much larger, something much stronger, something much more . . .

Gugs will hunt and kill without mercy.

If you ever, ever, for whatever reason, either dreaming or physically, find yourself in the city of the gugs, make sure you can run faster than your companions, as you could never outrun a gug. Shooting them with a pistol or throwing a spear at their chest will not halt them. Gugs just do not care about slight body wounds when in they are sport-hunting their favored meal of humans. Any gugs chasing you and your companions will close in on the slowest human they encounter. After killing, they then move on to the next slowest. The time they took in killing and sampling their prey enabled me to lose them in the cavern's murky distance.

If you and your comrades find yourself pursued by gugs, keep running, even if this is what the gugs want you to do, for you just may be able to outlast your companions in more ways than one. And I do know what will happen to you if are alone and hunted by gugs. I saw it once, as only once did I make the mistake of stopping and turning around when my last companion cried out to me for help, just before the gugs rent him limb from limb in a matter of seconds. Take my advice. If you don't wish to be ceaselessly tormented by such nightmarish images, remember to never, ever, look back, especially if you want to see how your companions are faring . . .

Gugs will hunt and kill without mercy.

Gugs will hunt and kill without mercy.

Gugs will hunt and kill without mercy.

Gugs will hunt and kill without mercy . . .

Hypnos: Say Yes to REM Sleep!

The god Hypnos has his influence on the Dreamlands and can extend his influence to Earth via dreams, as his realm of control is over those who dream deeply. Lovecraft wrote of Hypnos as a seemingly beneficial god who watches over humanity, but he is an alien god who is not of this Earth.

Sometimes he directs those terrestrial dreamers who wish to enter the Dreamlands.

Sometimes he doesn't.

Hypnos resembles a youthful Greek god of mythology, dressed in the attire appropriate to such a milieu. Such a vision of him is inspiring and awful (in the older sense of the word) at the same time. Hypnos grants the ability to those who dream to travel freely in all the Dreamlands and even into the dreams of other people. (Remember, when dreaming, one is free to explore the worlds in one's imagination, and sometimes one does wonder what others dreams of.) When the deity chooses a dreamer, Hypnos' smiling visage will appear to the dreamer and then the person will find themselves dreaming impossible scenes and emotions, as if the dreamer is pushing the limits of what the mind can comprehend or handle. Hypnos grants such powerful and awe-inspiring dreams, dreams that can only be feebly compared to the highest fantasies induced by opium and other terrestrial drugs.

This may sound like an ideal situation, but it is not.

Every one dreams, and when Hypnos selects a person, it is not one of weal for the dreamer. Like any strong narcotic, the dreams of Hypnos can take over the physical wants and needs of the person's body. Thus the dreamer becomes a shell, a junkie craving even more of the dreams, while the physical body is drained slowly of all vitality and health. This process can take weeks or months, depending on the person.

But where does the life force of the dreamer go when dreaming the dreams of Hypnos?

From the corpses left behind in the beds or alleys where dreamers selected by Hypnos dream their last, it would seem that Hypnos feeds upon the mortal life force of the dreamers he selects. Although one can resist his siren call, all must sleep; and in that sleep, Hypnos has sway . . . and sustenance.

Dream if you must, but dream only of that which comes naturally. The deep stage of REM sleep is where most people live out their dreams, and no other dreams can be as healthful as those. If you dream and see a young man's face with a noble visage and Mediterranean features, and a soft light emits from his forehead, do not go gently into the light. In fact, resist that light and do not go at all, for you may find yourself dreaming of escape, a release that will only come when you are tired.

Dead tired.

Leng Hounds with Wings: They Will Hound You . . . to Death!

Leng hounds are native to the Plateau of Leng, which is found in the Dreamlands. (Some scholars tend to believe the Plateau of Leng extends from the Dreamlands to our world, but that is a topic of some dispute, as the Plateau of Leng may exist in the Himalayas, or in Antarctica, or even under New York City . . .) Leng hounds do not have a strong social connection to the almost-humans of Leng, unlike the dogs of Earth with their strong connection to the human species. But it is known that the almost-humans of Leng, and sometimes human sorcerers, can utilize the Leng hounds as a mode of warding and/or revenge.

Revenge that knows neither limits of time nor extremes of distance.

Leng hounds are vaguely canine in appearance, and can grow to about the size of an earthly Great Dane. When I say "vaguely canine," I mean that if viewed from a distance (which I heartily recommend), a Leng hound resembles the profile of a dog: quadruped, long torso, head elevated above shoulders on a thick neck, and long-snouted face. But once you get closer, you can see that it is not a breed of dog one has ever seen on this Earth.

They have a variety of fur/skin colorations, just as the differing breeds of dogs on Earth do. Usually, the color scheme is dark colors, and their fur tends to run in the pattern that resembles camouflage—i.e., the color patterns tend to break up the silhouette of the hound, enabling it to stay hidden from view, even when out in the open. The muzzle is longer and filled with more teeth than a normal dog's, and the ears are rather bat-like (with serrated edges in some breeds) in appearance. The eyes glow an eerie crimson red or a baleful green, especially when the animal is sensing a kill. (This may just be an optical illusion, as Leng hounds usually attack in dark or near-dark situations, and any light used to illuminate these beasts just reflects the eyes, much like a cat's eyes will seem to glow in the dark when hit with a soft or weak light source.)

However, it is their wings that give away their identity. When not using them, Leng hounds will fold these wings along the long torsos on their back, so that the hound simply looks as though it has a thickened torso (or humpback) along the spine. When unfurled, the wings do not appear to be like any known avian appendage, but they do closely resemble a cross between a present-day bat wing and an ancient reptilian wing. The limb of the wings is covered in fur much like the rest of the hound's body. As for what covers the skin flap of the wing, I do not know, for the only people who have had the opportunity to examine such skin close up have perished, having been rent to death by the Leng hound's powerful jaws.

The Leng hound has a most dismaying cry. I have heard this baying roar a few times during my expeditions to haunted, out-of-the-way places. (Cemeteries seem to be the favorite spot for Leng hounds when they are on this Earth. See the next entry, about the almost-humans of Leng, for this data.) It may sound crazy, but I think the Leng hound's bay can shake one's very soul with its deep, resounding cries.

These bays strike fear and terror within the very essence of a person. (I also think this is why the almost-humans of Leng use these beasts.)

The Leng hounds will attack and tear their victims with teeth and claws, and according to the forensic evidence that has been found on corpses after these attacks, the hounds seem to shred and ingest portions of their victims. This would imply that they do feed upon meat, but what they tear off is the softest, most prime cuts of meat (if I may describe people in terms normally reserved for cattle).

Just as the almost-humans of Leng do with their human prey.

The almost-humans of Leng have powerful wizards and sorcerers among their numbers, and can conjure up and invoke a link to a Leng hound. Such a link is made to bind the hound to a certain object or person, to be that object's or person's watchdog—a guardian, if you will, for all eternity.

That means even from beyond the grave.

Leng hounds are horrific while alive, but gain ghastly powers when undead. They are able to track and detect their appointed ward across any distance of time or space. Being undead, a linked Leng hound will have all time it needs to complete its paranormal pursuit.

This is why you shouldn't steal things from graves. A Leng hound could be protecting that grave or its occupant.

I wonder what would happen if a ghoul robbed a grave that was guarded by a Leng hound. Who would win in that fight? Wouldn't that make a *fantastic* story?

Leng Almost-Humans: And You Thought the Hounds Were Terrible . . .

Just as deep ones come in two classifications, Leng almost-humans also come in two varieties: humanoid and can-pass-as-human. The true almost-human could not pass itself off as human under any circumstances; ones who pass as human only do so with certain types of clothing that conceal their nonhuman features.

Native to the Plateau of Leng in the Dreamlands (and feared and loathed their by the humans of that realm), the almost-humans greatly resemble the Greek mythological beings known as satyrs; indeed, it may be the almost-humans who gave rise to those legends, as the almost-humans used to trade in slaves with the ancient Greeks and Romans.

Pureblooded almost-humans walk upright, as humans do, but their legs are like a goat's, with large, cloven hooves. Thick, coarse, wiry hair covers their legs, torso, and upper arms, and male almost-humans have a dense beard growth, which they groom and allow to grow out. Their faces resemble a goat's in proportion: they have thin chins, large eyes, and tufted ears. Jutting from the forehead of almost-humans of either sex are horns, wrinkled, ringed, and curving like a terrestrial goat's. Their eyes are set too far apart for human sensibilities, and instead one imagines a goat face when gazing upon such a creature. Indeed, it is conjectured by this author that the Greek god Pan derives his stature and abilities from the almost-humans, as the sexual appetite of the almost-humans rivals that of the mythological deity. While the female of their species is not common, almost-humans have been known to seduce human females in order to propagate their own numbers. Normal humans and almost-humans can successfully reproduce.

This is why some Leng almost-humans can pass as human, because their features lean heavily toward their human parent. While all almost-humans retain the goat-like visage and legs of their species, some of these creatures can disguise or conceal their nonhuman attributes with certain styles of clothing. The almost-human's face is more humanlike in proportion, albeit they still retain the curly hair and beard, even among the females. Their skin tone will range from swarthy to sandy, similar to someone whose ancestors came from a desert region. The horns would be diminished in height, not reaching the full size of the pureblooded almost-humans, but those with horns small enough wear turbans to conceal the telltale growths. (Almost-humans wear hats of varying styles to conceal their forehead, but turbans offer the most securely attached headpiece, as the accidental dislodge of a disguised almost-human hat will surely be counterproductive to their evil machinations.)

Long, flowing robes and dresses help conceal their misshapen legs, and highly stylized high-heeled boots can be fitted over hooves that are more similar in size and outline to a human foot. Thus, in the Dreamlands, almost-humans in disguise will resemble any sort of person living in the desert culture of the Dreamlands, or humans from the desert region of North Africa, because of both their skin color and style of dress.

But why would almost-humans resort to such subterfuge? Simple. They are allied with the terrible toad-things, who originally hailed from Earth's Moon and have conquered the almost-humans. Centuries ago, the almost-humans waged war and won against their ancient foes, the Leng spiders (see the next entry), but the cunning almost-humans were later no match for the sheer brutality and efficiency of the toad-things' strategies. Recognizing the usefulness of almost-humans being able to pass themselves off as humans (something the toad-things could never do; see their entry in this book), the toad-things now utilize the almost-humans as the middlemen in the Dreamlands slave trade.

Indeed, the almost-humans stooped eagerly to their new role as slavers and artists of deception. With the wealth offered to them from the toad-things, the almost-humans ply their ships along the coast of the Dreamlands' seas, buying the choicest human slaves from the kingdoms there. The toad-things stay well hidden aboard their ships, but the almost-humans, garishly garbed with expensive robes and glittering with exquisite jewelry to bedazzle the eye, are greedily accepted into the cities by

154

those humans who fear the wrath of the toad-things and their nonhuman allies. For it is far better that some of your population be sold for profit than the entire culture be enslaved and carried off to the Moon for unspeakable tortures and labors.

At least, that's what the almost-humans whisper to the merchants when haggling over prices for trembling slaves.

The most prized bargaining tools the almost-humans possess are the massive rubies that the toad-things' slaves mine on the Moon. These rubies are the size of a man's fist on average, but examples have been sold that span many hand breadths; these are used as currency in some parts of the Dreamlands. Thus, the leering merchants who speak on behalf of the toad-things are tolerated in many port cities, as long as they, the almost-humans, behave themselves.

Over the centuries the almost-humans have learned many tricks of the slave trade from their repellent masters. Almost-humans have mastered the art of flattery and seduction in order to secure for themselves and their masters a bargain when it comes to haggling or bartering for slaves and other supplies. Preferring to use guile over brute force (perhaps due to the fact that the almost-humans cannot physically overthrow their Moon masters), the almost-humans can also slyly and craftily employ poisons, narcotics, and other drugs to enable their goals. It is not uncommon for a sailor to be offered a free glass of scented wine from a jolly merchant with too-wide eyes and a curious turban jeweled with rubies and gold, only for the sailor to later wake up with a splitting headache, chained to the railing of an almost-human galley.

Because of the prevalence of long robes and elaborate turbans among the human civilizations of the Dreamlands, it is not easy to distinguish an almost-human in disguise from any other type of Dreamlands human. One possible clue would be the gait of the merchant, as almost-humans prefer to go barefoot (bare-hoofed?); the click and clack of hooves upon a wooden surface is a sign that you should leave a bar or store immediately.

The almost-humans have learned many things from their devilish masters, and one skill they have acquired is the ability to season and roast meat, to enhance its natural flavor. Almost-humans have a gourmet secret (spices that are native only to the Plateau of Leng, along with rituals and incantations to alien gods, used in the preparation) that allows mouth-watering feasts to be prepared from an already sweet meat, the humans of Earth.

The almost-humans of Leng have developed a cult of eating human flesh.

Human flesh.

Since the almost-humans have traded with ancient Earth civilizations of the past, it would stand to reason that the almost-humans would still be trading with humans from Earth. While slavery has been legally abolished throughout the world, trafficking in humans as commodities still exists in many "civilized" nations of the world, including America. While robes and turbans may be an acceptable disguise in the Dreamlands, how would almost-humans disguise themselves in a modern, Western society? Would they wear, say, large cowboy hats to cover their horns and, say, ornate cowboy boots, with narrow feet and high heels, so they could walk on their hooves with little difficulty? Mayhap, disguised as laborers, they would wear hard hats with oversized rubber boots, so as not to attract attention. Or maybe elaborate hairdos, with bell-bottom pants?

I wonder . . .

Leng Spiders: Extreme Arachnophobia

If the spiders of Earth frighten you, do not go to the Plateau of Leng.

The spiders there would love to see you.

Once.

And then eat you.

Whole.

Once a populous race, the Leng spiders are becoming increasingly rare in the Dreamlands. Resembling a cross between an earthly web spider and a black widow, only on a much larger scale (a Leng spider can stand about five feet high and outstretch its lengthy limbs to about twelve feet across), Leng spiders are intelligent and crafty, nefarious by choice and also by fate. Their pendulous fangs are hung with several poison sacs to each fang; a Leng spider can deliver multiple lethal bites to multiple targets. It is rumored that each poison sac has its own unique chemical properties: some paralyze, some kill, others dissolve leather or metal.

Centuries ago, the almost-humans of Leng waged war with the spiders for control of certain habitable areas of the plateau. Why this war erupted, the exact causes for its beginnings, may never be known. Did the war happen before the almost-humans were enslaved by the toad-things? Or did it happen afterward? Knowing the war's exact dates could help pinpoint its possible causes, but the almost-humans are keeping quiet about their past war, as are the Leng spiders (not that anyone has seen one, much less sat down to talk with one, and then lived to tell the tale).

Outnumbering their hated foes, the almost-humans of Leng were victorious, and drove the remaining spiders deep into the crevices and crags of the mountains, or into the most deep and desolate of woodlands. Scattered now, the spiders of Leng live in quiet desperation, as they yearn to one day reclaim their birth lands. Their numbers have dwindled; living in exile has not helped the propagation of their species. But why were these monsters beaten in open warfare?

I think one reason for their defeat is that the Leng spiders are bound (no pun intended) to the webs they spin. Wherever the almost-humans found a web lair of a Leng spider, they could easily destroy the web with a few, well-placed flaming arrows. The spiders, unable to overcome the range advantage of their simian-like competitors, fell as easy targets to the archers and their flame strikes. If not burned alive in their homes, they were burned out of their homes, and a spider without a web cannot easily feed itself. Attacking an almost-human city was a Pyrrhic victory for the spiders, as the almost-humans could escape on ships if need be, and rebuilding destroyed masonry and timbers was easier with the help of slaves. The Leng spiders had nowhere to retreat if their homes were attacked, and any repairs came from the bodies of the spiders themselves. If a spider was injured, its ability to spin a web was limited, and therefore its shelter and means of acquiring food was limited.

Not much else is known about these gigantic spiders now. Travelers returning from the Plateau of Leng do not have any stories about encountering these monsters in the wild. Does this mean the Leng spiders are extinct? No, because travelers and explorers *do* report finding newly abandoned web lairs and dead, desiccated animals (such as horses or elephants), which would indicate the activities of these spiders are continuing. I would put forth the hypothesis that no one has reported seeing a Leng spider in the wild because Leng spiders make sure that there are no survivors of any who cross into their territories and behold their purplish bodies. And since their exact territory is not known (only deduced from tracks, debris, and webs), I would guess these spiders have in their diet their fair share of blissfully ignorant Earth dreamers and Dreamlands humans.

Since the almost-humans of Leng were able to defeat the spiders using long-range weaponry, and thus avoid hand-to-hand fighting that could have resulted in casualties to their kind, and since no one has reported seeing a living Leng spider, I put forth another hypothesis: the Leng spiders have developed the art of camouflage and traps to capture their prey. Some spiders on Earth, like the trap-door spider, will camouflage their burrow with a cunning door that blends in easily with its surroundings. I have seen these trap-door spiders in action. They spread out radiating weblines on the soil or flora outside their lairs. These weblines act as sensor devices, just like a motion detector in home security systems. Anytime something (or someone!) crosses or touches these weblines, a signal is sent back to the spider in its lair. The spider doesn't have to actually see its prey; it can make an educated guess as to the actual location of the trespasser, and how big it is. A trap-door spider will not attack anything triggering these weblines that is bigger than itself, but I am guessing the Leng spiders have no such compunction. A hapless traveler or animal on the Plains of Leng might never see the hidden trapdoor open up behind it, nor ever see the gleam in the Leng spider's myriad eyes as it sinks its poisoned fangs into its prey's back.

And since the Leng spiders are intelligent, what is to say that they don't set their traps with bait? A pile of shiny coins or some glittering gems, innocently looking as if they were accidentally dropped from a careless merchant's pouch, would make a tempting prize for any human. Even a pool of clear water would be a welcome sight to a weary traveler, only if the traveler doesn't notice the string of fine lines rounding the water's edge—fine lines that if followed point to a single origin, which disappears into the rocky ground. . . .

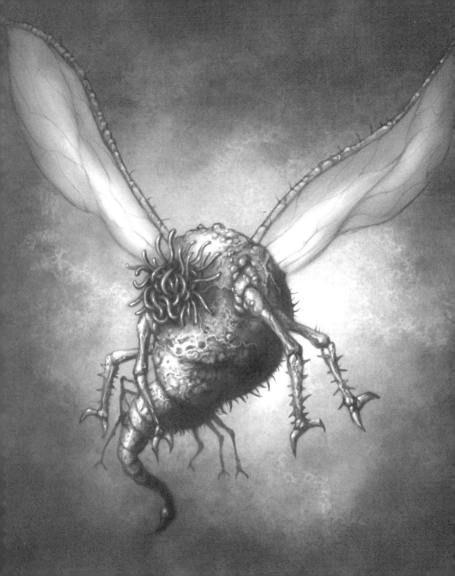

Mi-Goes: Pluto's Nasty Secret

Hmm, mi-goes. The name is pronounced *mee-goes*. *Mi-goes* is the plural term; *mi-go* is the singular form. You will rarely if ever encounter just one mi-go, as they tend to travel in swarms. They're alien monsters. Not even human-looking. Oh sure, you can kill one with a well-placed shotgun blast, but what good will that do when you are heavily outnumbered and all you have with you is your brain . . .

Mi-goes are a race of beings whose home world is called Yuggoth, which humans now know as the planet Pluto. Possessing great intelligence and advanced technology, mi-goes travel bodily through space via an unknown propulsion energy activated by their wings. They have no need for spacesuits or spacecraft; as their bodies are toughened and conditioned to travel in the cold vacuum of outer space and/or the warm rainforests of the tropics. In fact, some mi-goes have formed a colony in the Himalayas of Nepal; natives there who have been fortunate enough to see such creatures (and live to talk about them) have called them "abominable snowmen," which is confusing when describing what a mi-go actually looks like.

Let's talk more about their bodies.

The body of the mi-go is analogous to the body of a lobster, with a vaguely crustacean appearance to their carapaced body, but imagine if the lobster had evolved from plant life instead of animal life, and if the lobster was dead, soaking in sea water for days. A live mi-go's normal coloration is pink; dead mi-goes have been known to take a paler pink or whitish hue before disintegrating slowly in the sunlight. (Being from an alien world, mi-goes have a possible chemical and biological composition in their bodies that makes their bodies immune or insusceptible, except after death, to most kinds of energies or radiation found under the yellow sun of Earth.)

Coursing through their bodies is a greenish liquid, which acts as blood. The adult mi-go's body is about five feet long, from the tip of its flattened tail to its "head," which consists of a myriad of short antennae. Wings run along the mi-go's back, which can span ten feet or more in total length. Eyewitnesses have reported that the mi-go's external "skin" resembles a mottled or decomposing hubris of plant life.

I think that is where the plant analogy works when trying to visualize these creatures. Does your mind picture a bloated lobster sprinkled with rotting vegetation?

Each mi-go has two predominate limbs nearest its head region, and these appendages act as arms to manipulate objects. Along the course of the trunk are symmetrically placed lower legs, which can number anywhere from six to ten depending on the species. Pincers, about six inches long, are at the end of each of the limbs, and the mi-goes are able to grasp dexterously with any pincer, albeit the front two pincers are favored to handle most physical chores.

Mi-goes are very social with one another, but tend to shy away from groups of humans, preferring to remain unseen. The natural language of the mi-goes is a thin, buzzing sound made from vocal cords in their head region. This language greatly resembles the buzzing of earthly insects at night, which has caused some outdoor campers to theorize that perhaps the noisy "swarm of mosquitoes" they heard all night wasn't responsible for the tracks in the mud around their tents.

Mi-goes will also communicate via "facial" colorations, along with bodily movements (think of a honeybee reporting back to the hive and disclosing the location of a savory flower bed via a specialized dance that shows the location of the flowers to others). Because of the mi-goes' buzzing sounds, and their appearance and certain mannerisms while "dancing," an insect analogy does help here to understand the appearance of said beings.

Sighting a mi-go in real life can cause you to question your reality.

In outer space, mi-goes flap their wings to sail into the ether; it has been theorized they either use solar winds or some sort of unknown element to hurtle themselves though the void. In terrestrial settings, a mi-go can clumsily fly short distances, and have been observed sailing the skies in packs or singly in daylight or at night. Because of their clumsy and imprecise control of their wings in our atmosphere, walking is the mi-go's preferred mode of transport while on Earth (which accounts for the large number of claw prints wherever mi-goes live).

Oh yes, mi-goes successfully live on Earth. Pluto may be their homeworld, but many mi-goes now call Earth their home. Mi-goes may travel via the help of Yog-Sothoth, the god also known as the Keeper of the Gate, as certain occult sources name the mi-goes as one race that worships Yog-Sothoth because they may travel extensively using these doorways that Yog-Sothoth opens.

Favoring secluded regions of Earth's geography that can offer precious minerals and other needed metals without the intrusion of humanity's attentions, mi-goes have come to our planet to mine and refine the natural materials here.

This seems like an innocent endeavor.

Did I mention they collect heads? Human heads.

More specifically, they collect what is inside those human heads.

Mi-goes, being from an alien world, prefer to nourish themselves on foodstuffs native to Yuggoth. While mi-goes have been known to explore and settle on other worlds besides Earth and Pluto, they still depend on supplies from Yuggoth. Supply caravans travel from Yuggoth/Pluto to feed the growing number of mi-goes living on Earth, and the foodstuff is transported in metallic tins carried on the mi-goes' bodies. There have never been any, any whatsoever, reports of mi-goes feeding on terrestrial plants or animals, including human heads.

Hey, were you thinking they would be eating human heads!? What in the world would you think that? Oh, I see . . .

Mi-goes have an sophisticated culture and (compared to humans) greatly advanced science, which allows them to use surgery or metallurgy to create fantastic (to human sensibilities) devices. Mi-goes, as curious scientists, have been known to kidnap the minds of intelligent creatures they encounter during their travels in outer space, skillfully removing the brains and storing them in a metal canisters, which are able to survive the vacuum of outer space. These brain cylinders are outfitted to be readily attached to various machines to mimic the natural voice of the brain's host body.

Also with surgery, mi-goes have been known to mimic human beings in appearance and mannerisms. As they are inhuman, however, they cannot fully mimic human emotions or mannerisms. (Imagine watching a human in a gorilla suit. No matter how realistic the makeup and suit has been rendered, there still is some small clue in the "gorilla" movements that gives away the "human" inside, as the human does not know the exact mindset of a gorilla, nor are the bodily movements similar to those that are instinctive for a gorilla.)

Surgeons in the mi-go hive can alter the vocal chords of their own kind to make their language more human-sounding, but with surgery alone the best that mi-goes can hope for is a whiny, high-pitched voice that will buzz at odd times. Mi-goes decide to alter their voices in order to talk directly to humans (although usually the mi-goes who do so remain hidden from view, and so generally such talks are conducted at night). When questioned on the odd quality of their voice, a clever mi-go might comment that they are sick (with laryngitis or a cold) or are from a foreign land (with a "thick accent").

Nowadays, mi-goes favor making contact with humans on devices such as telephones or ham radios; in this way, the mi-goes can remain out of sight and their odd vocal quality can be attributed to the electronic device used or poor reception. (The sight of a mi-go can cause one to question reality, remember!) Again, no matter how humanlike the voice is, there is always something that can be a clue to the nonhuman nature of the speaker (once you learn what those vocal intonations and peculiarities are, that is!). The Internet is a device that Lovecraft could not have dreamed of, but one that the mi-goes could easily adapt for communication with humans. (Think of who might be sending that very odd-sounding e-mail the next time you look into your spam folder!)

Curious about other species, but with the curiosity of emotionless, scientific observers, mi-goes store on their home world of Yuggoth a large collection of the brains they have collected across the galaxy. There, mi-go scribes will attach speaking and recording devices to the brain canisters they select, and then archive that knowledge in their vast libraries. Thus, any knowledge, no matter how trivial, is kept on file on the Yuggothian world. And that information is distributed freely, as the mi-goes are of a hive mind, and knowledge is transmitted naturally and easily. This is another reason why you will never usually see just one mi-go; being of a hive mind, they prefer the company of others of their own kind. Where there is one mi-go, there are more . . .

Mi-goes also travel in human society, surgically altered as well as they can so that they can pass themselves off as human.

These disguised aliens are closely monitoring and recording human behavior up close, in order to add to their vast repository of knowledge. Such researchers/infiltrators would most likely be outfitted with latex or rubber masks on their faces and wearing bulky clothing to conceal aspects of their bodies that might arouse curiosity or concern. (This may account for the description of mi-goes in Nepal as "abominable snowmen.") Such in-depth research is dangerous for the mi-goes, who value privacy and a lack of interest from their human subjects. Mi-goes can never truly pass as being human, so there is always the chance a disguise may fall away, or that a mannerism may reveal itself as being most odd . . .

In their sciences the mi-goes do have a stupendous arsenal of weaponry, most of it never used since their last wars with the Cthulhu spawn and the elder things, which occurred millennia before even the dinosaurs roamed the fetid Earth. These weapons they will not dare use, for while they value the safety of their numbers, the mi-goes will not risk an all-out war with their ancient foes or even the primitive but nuclear-armed monkey savages of Earth, which would thus possibly deprive themselves of a rich treasure trove like the one our planet offers to them. Instead, mi-goes will work quietly behind the scenes, living in places not inhabited by humans, but always eager to keep updated on the advances of human technology or philosophy. Mi-goes prefer to remain unknown by the population at large, but paradoxically they will reveal themselves to select individuals whom they find mentally intriguing.

While quite tough physically, mi-goes have been known to die from the same causes that can kill humans, notably a blast of buckshot from a shotgun. Such occurrences are rare, as mi-goes are very careful to avoid human attention. They know humans are dangerous but intelligent.

Mi-goes. They love the gray matter that humans use. So much so that they will collect human brains and place them in jars to display on library shelves, even if that library is on a planet millions of miles from Earth.

On a side note, the planet Pluto was "discovered" by humans in 1930, which caused a great stir in the human scientific community. Then, in the early twenty-first century, Pluto was reclassified by astronomers as something less than a planet, and was therefore relegated as a lesser body in the Earth's solar system.

Since mi-goes want to remain hidden from earthlings' knowledge, the discovery of their planet Yuggoth must have triggered an investigation into how they could remain unknown. Because Earth's astronomers and their telescopes have already found and photographed their home world, this knowledge cannot be erased from human memory. I am guessing that the mi-go scientists, in their study of the wrinkled brains and convoluted mental activities of humans, found the best way to avoid detection from snooping humans was to become inconsequential to their monkey-like specimens. I wonder how many "astronomers" who urged others to reclassify Pluto were actually people, and not some mi-go in a human suit!

Moon's Toad-Things:
Toadies of Torture

Dwelling natively on the dark-side surface of Earth's Moon, the toad-things are truly repellent to behold, for their squishy, pasty bodies expand and contract at will, protean, causing the human eye to dizzy at their sight.

Toad-things derive their name from their toad-like bodies; they have four limbs, with the two in front shorter then the rear two. However, toad-things have no head; where you might expect one to be is only a mass of lengthy tentacles centered on a pinkish snout. No eyes are visible, nor are any needed, as toad-things sense sound vibrations via snouted tentacles. And fear. Toad-things love the tender psychic pulses of fear. Humans produce such pulses. And toad-things think humans produce the best pulses when tortured . . .

Toad-things stand roughly five feet tall at the shoulder/head region, but this height will shift easily as they are protean. Some toad-things have been reported with sizes far larger and far smaller than this. Their four legs have feet/hands that are as webbed as an earthly toad's, with four "fingers" and one "thumb" on a foot; each digit terminates in a hooked claw. Each hand has six digits, with a symmetrically placed "thumb" placed at either side of four "fingers."

Toad-things do not wear any clothes, but are highly intelligent and cruel. Any adornments they might wear would be for the carrying of instruments of torture. Toad-things are slave owners and slave traders, hiring the fiendish almost-humans of Leng to act as their middle "men" (forgive my intentional pun). Slaves that are favored are the human races of both the Dreamlands and the Earth. Traveling in multi-banked galleys tarred black in color, toad-things and their allies ride upon the oceans waves in both worlds, freely traveling between the two realms on moonlit currents. Prizing the healthiest and fattest humans as prey, the almost-humans of

Leng reap considerable wealth when supplying such "trade goods" to their inhuman (and inhumane) employers.

Toad-things will pay their employees with rubies that are only found on the Moon, rubies that are enormous when compared to the pitiful size of earthly gems, rubies so large that they can be carved into goblets and used for drinking. The almost-humans of Leng will use such rubies to entice humans to their black-colored ships, as the lure of such treasures can bend the will of even the most prudent or most pauperized of persons, and those with the plumpest physiques or bulging with muscles will be considered the most savory by the toad-things. The almost-humans of Leng will offer such rubies to particular people, with the promise of more to come if only they will step aboard their ship . . .

With such treasures, the almost-humans of Leng do not need to use violence to secure their "trade goods," as their cattle will line up in the pens and corrals they install on their ships. If the treasures do not work, the toad-things know of many sedatives and intoxicants one can place into a drink, drugs that make even the strongest easily succumb to sleep.

Most secretive, toad-things will remain hidden from view when their ships arrive in ports, and none but their most trusted servants are allowed to view their ceremonies or private lives. For the most part, nothing for certain is known about the toad-things, save that they are originally from the dark side of the Moon and have an immense city there, and they have been steadily strengthening their influence and presence along the merchant routes of the Dreamlands.

I have heard from travelers and the denizens of the Dreamlands that toad-things are rumored to eat the fattened human slaves they acquire, but this is unproven, as no person has actually seen such a meal. (But it may be true, because any humans who witnessed such a meal would have been the main course . . .) But it is more likely that toad-things feed upon the psychic horror and terror that torture can produce, as the toad-things have developed torture to such a high art form. Beings who run afoul of the toad-things have been heard screaming for days, as the toad-things ply their trade behind gauze tents within sight of a terrified populace.

Woe to any person captured by the toad-things. It is something I would not wish upon my most hated enemy.

A toad-thing's tentacles on its "face" are extremely sensitive to pain, so if you find yourself being taken away by these brutes, you would be well advised to aim your blows at these tentacles. However, one has to be in a position to be able to flee from such a beast, for I have heard stories about people who have resisted thusly, only to find themselves the subject of particularly gruesome torture inflicted the toad-things.

Since the tarred galleys of the toad-things and their allies can travel from the Moon to the Dreamlands, and travel is also possible from the Dreamlands to Earth, it bothers me that the toad-things may be extending their slave-trading activities. Ships that disappear in the ocean expanses have been reported for centuries: could the toad-things be partly responsible? Also, thousands of people go missing every year. I wonder how many people disappear from the port cities that sprawl across the shores of our great oceans, oceans that in certain areas can stretch to the oceans of the Dreamlands. And as American culture cultivates the impossibly muscular body ideal yet has an increasing obesity epidemic, would not the American people be the ideal "goods" that the toad-things crave?

If you travel to any city that overlooks the sea, it is best not to yield to any admonitions from strangely garbed people who do not let you see their employers but will use impossible treasures as promises of more to come, if only you will grace their ship in the harbor for a secret meeting . . .

Necronomicon:
Do Not Open . . .
Except in Case of Emergency!

The *Necronomicon*, technically, is not a monster, and it most definitely is not a living creature. The *Necronomicon* is a book. However, it is a book that never was meant to be, but does exist; a tome that should not be read, but must be; a book that induces madness, but, umm, well, it really *does* induce insanity and despair.

One of Lovecraft's more famous creations (or infamous, depending on your moral relativism concerning arcane lore), the *Necronomicon* was written by the mad author Abdul Alhazred. When I say *mad*, I don't mean "upset" or "angry," but the type of *mad* that indicates a mental breakdown or unstable thoughts.

Believed to be originally written about 738 CE, possibly in Yemen (where Abdul Alhazred lived), the *Necronomicon*'s original title was *Al Azif*. This title, in Arabic, was supposed to be indicative of the whirring sounds insects make nocturnally while in the wastes of the deserts, noises that are actually the voices of demons as they talk. (If a mental alarm is raised as you read this, then go back and take a look at the chapter on mi-goes and the description of their oral communications . . .)

The *Al Azif*, written in Arabic, was later published in Latin and retitled as the *Necronomicon*. It has been translated into many different languages throughout the centuries, but the *Necronomicon* version of *Al Azif* is by far the most widespread version of the book, since, well, *Al Azif* is not known to exist anymore. By the late seventeenth century, the invention of the printing press had made possible the widespread availability to the public of copies of the *Necronomicon*, whereas *Al Azif* was a series of handwritten parchment bundles. By the way, Lovecraft did not read or write Arabic, so his knowledge of Arabic names was rather limited and inaccurate. Language scholars may note that the names *Abdul Alhazred* and *Al Azif* are linguistically incorrect. But scholars are known to be wrong, as they also don't believe in words like *Cthulhu* or *mi-goes*.

The *Necronomicon* has had a long history of suppression by the dominant cultural forces of the time. From the Arabic of the original *Al Azif*, the book has been translated into Latin, Greek, English, and French, and each of these translations was once widely distributed. But with each publication came the ban of its reading by moral and religious forces, who deemed the book a harbinger of evil and proclaimed that those who would dare read such blasphemies should be put to death. Beginning in the early Middle Ages, the *Necronomicon* was banned and burned wherever it was found. Only because of the fortitude of certain scholars of the occult do editions still exist. The *Necronomicon*, for, example, is no longer found as a compete text, as each surviving book has had passages or pages removed and destroyed. Thus, in order to read the entire book, one must find each edition (usually in deplorable shape from centuries of use and abuse) and read through the different translations, as each version might not contain a section found in other versions.

But what is written in the *Necronomicon* to make it so shocking, so maddeningly fatiguing to comprehend? According to

Lovecraft, the *Necronomicon* was filled all sorts of lore, reference, trivia, knowledge, and occult information pertaining to the monsters, demons, and deities of the Mythos. The *Necronomicon* is a Who's Who of the Mythos. Characters in Lovecraft's stories who have read the *Necronomicon* may find certain passages of the text alarmingly true when, for example, encountering a monster that does not fit any previously known description, but one that fits the ramblings of the mad Abdul Alhazred in his famous book. Also, there is no index, no table of contents, no seeming semblance of any order to how the text appears. Passages on a particular subject might suddenly end mid-paragraph, then continue abruptly scores of pages later.

This book is simply the ranting of a madman, a madman who had moments of clarity. Such lucid passages are far and few between, and it is left up to the reader to make sense of the whole. Each passage is a part of a puzzle, albeit some of the puzzle pieces are not the ones the reader is trying to solve, which adds to the frustrating and "maddening" traits of the writings within the *Necronomicon*.

Nor are the writings within the *Necronomicon* for the faint-hearted. Inside its pages are tales of the true nature of the universes, a nature that dampens and withers the ardor of the human spirit. According to the *Necronomicon*, the gods of Earth that mortal men worship are merely feeble-minded and frail-bodied children compared to the powers of the Elder Gods, those alien beings that came from the stars to claim Earth as their own. These Elder Gods do not reign supreme now, but will one day again do so, until then allowing the humans to worship their puny deities. But to hasten the day when the Elder Gods regain their rightful throne/yoke over Earth, the *Necronomicon* instructs the reader about how to contact these gods, including Cthulhu and Yog-Sothoth, to beseech their aid and activate their powers.

What the Elder Gods desire most is to be able to return to Earth in triumph, and much of the lore in the *Necronomicon* is about just how exactly to let these monsters in. The *Necronomicon* is a recipe book for cooking up and contacting most of the creatures described in this primer you are reading, complete with how-to steps and philosophical insights about how such beings work and operate. Mind you, the formulas and recipes are not neatly spelled out, nor do they have ingredients that are readily available, but the spells and recipes offer incredible powers to those knowledgeable or skillful enough to rouse the forgotten but ever-near Elder Gods.

That's why the book was banned for many centuries and was fervently suppressed, for no one would want to invite in the Elder Gods. No sane person, that is. The *Necronomicon* might just appeal to the twisted logic of someone insane, someone under the influence of an alien mindset . . . oops, did I just write that down? Disregard that last sentence; no alien in their right mind would ever want a human read the *Necronomicon*, as it would only lead to the human's mental collapse, and not possibly even further the goals and machinations of the aliens, such as the mi-goes, elder things, deep ones, or any of the gods mentioned in this humble primer. No way, no how, would any alien mind would ever want to influence a human to read the *Necronomicon*.

You have my assurances on that!

This leads me to another point, as to why exactly some characters in Lovecraft's stories willingly read the *Necronomicon*. These characters need to understand the insanity, the illogical, the impossible around them. When a horrific monster appears, and neither bullets nor fire stop the creature, certain occult scholars need to be able to utilize any knowledge base at hand to combat this scourge, and one such database is the *Necronomicon*. A person of stern mental constitution would be able to read, comprehend, and internalize the contents of the *Necronomicon* without succumbing to the collapse of one's own mind, an internal collapse that would shield the person from further understanding of the uncaring and hostile cosmos.

One of the supposed weals of the *Necronomicon* is the use of the Elder Sign, a sigil when properly constructed and displayed that will repel even the most dread of gods, Cthulhu. With such lore gleaned from the *Necronomicon*, some people have been able to defeat or thwart the machinations of Cthulhu and other such evil deities. But such a person is rare indeed. If one's mind does comprehend the insanity within the *Necronomicon*, the strain of knowing may be taking a toll physically on that person. People under mental strain undergo physical ailments, such as a weakened constitution or acceleration of infirmities that were previously not life-threatening. One way or the other, the *Necronomicon* exacts a price from its readers.

That's why I said that the book should never be opened. That is, except in case of an emergency, and it has to be a great emergency indeed. Such emergencies would include living next door to a active warren of ghouls who are threatening to dig their way into your basement while you sleep, or your next-door neighbor trying to summon Yog-Sothoth and becoming successful at summoning this entity's powers when the stars grow dark and the wind howls abysmally cold . . .

Book dealers and occult students will tell you the *Necronomicon* is a figment of the imagination of a short-lived American horror writer and that no such book ever existed. But how is it that you can search a bookstore and find an actual copy of it on the shelves? Don't believe me? Go down to your local library and look up this book. Better yet, go on the Internet and do a search for it. Chances are you will find scores of these books for sale, some at rather affordable prices. This contradiction, how an imagined book became a honest-to-goodness tome, is one of the magics of the Mythos—to make real what is supposedly "unreal."

Lovecraft insisted the *Necronomicon* was entirely make-believe, but he wanted his readers to believe it was a real book, to lend verisimilitude to his tales. After all, what could be more terrifying than reading about a character in a book who makes reference to a book in the real world, particularly one the reader has even read previously? (Remember my lecture on what is real and what isn't?) But some of Lovecraft's core fans insisted that such a book must exist, as Lovecraft did cite actual books in his stories, books known to scholars and the general public, such as *The Wonders of the Invisible World* by Cotton Mather and *The Witch-Cult in Western Europe* by Margaret Murray. And most damning of all, Lovecraft wrote an essay of the history of the *Necronomicon*, citing a Latin translation of the *Necronomicon* by one Olaus Wormius, a famous (and historically verifiable) person who lived in seventeenth-century Denmark. This history, said some of his fans, is proof enough that the *Necronomicon* exists. After all, why would a writer create a work of nonfiction when he normally writes fiction? I urge the reader to find a copy of Lovecraft's essay "The History of the *Necronomicon*," and carefully look at the names of the early translators. I think doing so will answer that last question.

Then, in the 1960s, patrons of libraries began to ask librarians about finding a copy of the *Necronomicon*, which, of course, did not show up on any card catalogs. (Remember, electronic cataloging of books is a recent development; prior to the computer, information about library holdings was stored on index cards in filing cabinets.) Librarians were frustrated with these ridiculous requests, and things turned even weirder as practical jokers inserted faked entries for the *Necronomicon* into card catalogs, which caused even more confusion. Librarians insisted the book had never existed. Fans of Lovecraft had read the selfsame negative declarations by librarians in his stories; being a banned book, surely these modern denials showed the book was being suppressed? And as more interest grew in the Mythos, authors began to incorporate the *Necronomicon* into their own works, adding to the puzzle. (If you are curious, look at the bibliography in Michael Crichton's novel *Eaters of the Dead* to see what I mean!)

Then, in the 1970s, a mainstream press published a paperback copy of a book titled *The Necronomicon*. Fans and non-fans were delighted to finally be able to read this forbidden book; librarians were also delighted as now their card catalogs were accurate. This book, however, was simply a retelling of *The Descent of Inanna into the Underworld*, an ancient Sumerian text (real, not fake!), with the names of Lovecraft's monsters and deities thrown into the mix.

Does your head hurt? Think you might be losing your grip on reality? Now you understand. Shockingly, but at least you understand.

The popularity of Lovecraft's works now makes for a wider audience, and various publishers have printed an actual *Necro-*

nomicon for the fans' enjoyment; many authors have taken up the challenge and penned a copy of Abdul Alhazred's most famous work. The *Necronomicon* now does exist in print, in several languages, and some versions do inspire the crazed terror and fear as described in the actual *Necronomicon*, as these writers are as skilled as Lovecraft in creating an atmosphere of gloom, horror, and cosmic dread.

Do you think I am brilliantly insane, or am I insanely brilliant, for pointing out the "fantasy" of Lovecraft is *actually* the "reality" of Lovecraft?

Remember, I have a signed document that states I am certifiably *not* insane.

Night-Gaunts: Ticklish Terrors for Travelers

A night-gaunt is a humanoid creature, about six to eight feet tall, that resembles a horned demon of Christian mythology. Indeed, a night-gaunt is humanoid in body, but has large, bat-like wings and a set of horns protruding from either side of its head. A barbed tail further cements the allusion to the demon of lore, and the entire skin of the night-gaunt is inky black, oily, as if a living shadow. Night-gaunts are sexless, and have no faces whatsoever.

Night-gaunts have no faces.

The front of a night-gaunt's head is smooth, with slight angles to suggest a forehead and chin, but the rest of that blank face is simply not suggested at all. Night-gaunts do not see with any sensory organ known to humanity; instead, they are able to perceive vision all around them through their skin, and are able to see in the blackest of nights. This suggests they are able to see into more than just the visible light spectrum, but night-gaunts prefer to dwell and hunt in the dark of the night. Without a face, it is horribly clear that night-gaunts cannot eat or drink, and what the night-gaunts sustain themselves with is unknown.

Night-gaunts do not seem to possess an intelligence higher than that of an average dog, as it is known that night-gaunts do not have a spoken language of their own but can react and learn limited commands when they are taught and commanded to do so. Some travelers in the Dreamlands have, with limited success, learned to use night-gaunts as a steed, but it is a very rare night-gaunt indeed that can be "domesticated" in such a way. The mere inhospitality of their lairs makes for a species that normally has little chance for interactions with other species, adding to the difficulties in the attempt.

Night-gaunts are native to the mountainous regions of the Dreamlands, where they keep aeries high atop inaccessible mountain peaks. Immune to cold and heat, this location serves the night-gaunts best as a natural defense against any being or creature who might disturb them. As I said, night-gaunts behave as if they have no refined intelligence save that of an animal instinct. Normally keeping to themselves and not bothering anyone or anything else, night-gaunts will occasionally fly down from their perches and seek out victims. This "kidnapping" doesn't seem to be a normal activity for the night-gaunts, however, and is very atypical of their normal behavior, which is to avoid contact with other beings.

In these potentially harmful situations, night-gaunts have been known to act as if guided by a superior mind. They are known to kidnap earthly dreamers who spend their non-waking moments in the Dreamlands, or any Dreamlands humans who dare to walk alone, or else they fly in the skies of the Dreamlands, attacking steed or perch in order to secure their quarry. For what purpose the night-gaunts abduct people is not known, as sometimes the night-gaunt will dislodge a human from its mount (it can be a land-bound steed, like a horse or mule, or even an airborne steed, like a roc or any other type of large bird utilized in the Dreamlands for transport, but not the shantak-bird, as these creatures are terrified by the smell or sight of night-gaunts, and will flee from the ebony-skinned monsters). The night-gaunt will snatch the human into the air and carry them away toward a remote destination, usually in the mountains or some other forsaken place uninhabited by humans.

Needless to say, there is much screaming and shouting by the unfortunate victim, made all the more horrifying because the night-gaunt is silent and stony in its expression. Remember, night-gaunts have no faces, but they will turn their heads and face their victims, as if understanding the contents of the humans' screams or cries for help. But no amount of screaming or pleading will result in a release from their grips.

Of course, some people resist such a capture and abduction, but the night-gaunts are strong, capable of clasping and restraining a fully grown human male while still flying at abnormal speeds. If the human resists, the night-gaunt will tickle its burden, with increasing agility and speed, until the human ceases to resist. This tickling is methodical and unyielding. If the human continues to resist, the night-gaunt uses its barbed tail to further tickle and torment its load. This tickling can be done at any stage of the abduction, from the initial contact all the way until the journey's end.

Because of their oily black pigmentation, it is very difficult to see a night-gaunt at night, but any sort of moon, star, or torchlight reflects easily on its ebony epidermis.

A night-gaunt can travel for miles tirelessly and unwaveringly at breakneck speed. If the human resists too strongly, or is somehow immune to the fiendish tickling due to layering or thickness of clothing, the night-gaunt will soar upward into the atmosphere, then drop its human prey, who plunges screaming and kicking toward the impatient ground. Before the human actually hits the waiting earth, the night-gaunt will swoop down and snatch the hapless person at the last possible moment. This terrifying sequence can be repeated until the victim becomes subdued (either through exhaustion or fainting), and the night-gaunt will now journey on with no further pesky interruptions.

Because of the speed at which a night-gaunt flies, a person could develop frostbite rather easily at higher altitudes in cooler climates, but night-gaunts do not seem to be interested in allowing their human cargo to be damaged, and will protect their loads from the elements. This fact is odd, and it causes many scholars of the Dreamlands to ponder the mystery of the night-gaunts.

Why does the night-gaunt abduct people? Since the night-gaunts do not use tools or have any indication of a civilization, and live in remote, inhabitable places, it is assumed (by the scholars of the Dreamlands) that night-gaunts are mere beasts of burden, somehow guided by a higher but outside intelligence. It has been theorized that night-gaunts are in thrall to Nyarlathotep, the most evil god, one of whose many descriptions is a human male figure whose skins and facial features (including eyes) are inky black in color; these physical colorings and seemingly random kidnappings would indeed suggest a link.

Yet according to wizened sages and occult scholars of the Dreamlands, night-gaunts are actually favored by Nodens, the deity of dreamers in the Dreamlands and on Earth (see the next entry). Random kidnappings, with no discernible purpose save to confound the traveler from reaching her dreams/goals would appear to be the purpose of the night-gaunts' activities. Indeed, the night-gaunt will seek not to harm its prey, but will drop them off on an unscalable peak or in the middle of a wasteland and fly away, leaving the humans to fend for themselves. Nodens will guard these dreamers and worshippers, so perhaps he is sending the night-gaunts to carry his wards away from potential danger, but is failing to instruct the mindless night-gaunts exactly where to safely land their charges. Or perhaps there is another intelligence at work here, mayhap another one the of the gods of the Dreamlands, one with a less benevolent intention . . .

Lovecraft himself saw night-gaunts. Night-gaunts aren't just a literary creation of his. As a child, he was tormented in his nightmares by faceless ebony demons that flew through the air. As a way of coping with these terrifying dream creatures, he wrote about them in the stories that make up the *Dream-Quest of Unknown Kadath* collection, stories that center around the adventures of the character Randolph Carter as he travels to and from the Dreamlands. Night-gaunts are terrible and awesome to Randolph, and through the stories we get glimpses of these creatures. Perhaps this writing was therapeutic for Lovecraft, as he was able to relate to others the harrowing adventures he had as a dreaming child.

Or perhaps Lovecraft was trying to alert us that night-gaunts actually do exist . . .

Nodens: Just Say No to Slumber . . .

A god of the Dreamlands, Nodens has been known to favor or aid dreamers in their journeys, but like most deities of the Dreamlands, his intentions may not seem beneficial or desirable at all. Appearing to both dreamers and those wide awake as a heroic man with a mane of white hair and a ponderous beard, Nodens is known as the Lord of the Abyss, and he travels atop a platform made from a huge seashell carried on the backs of dolphins.

The Abyss is the gulf between the sleeping and the awake, the unconscious and the conscious.

Nodens will willingly lend his aid to any dreamer who asks for it, or who he finds in need of assistance, as he freely travels between the Dreamlands and the Waking World. Think of Nodens as an interdimensional Boy Scout, eager to help you cross the road—the road in this case being the one between the land of Nod and the land of alertness.

Like felines, Nodens will act as a beneficial guide to the traveler and be a most willing host. Ask him questions you may have about the Dreamlands and the dream itself, for he is wise and filled with the knowledge of all the dreamers he has helped. But it should be known that the night-gaunts, those faceless demons of the skies, are said to be at the behest of Nodens. While terrifying and devilish in appearance and mannerisms, night-gaunts at first glance do not appear to be the agent of any rewarding god, and rightly so. Dreamers who find themselves whisked away by night-gaunts often have nightmares in their dreams about these beasts and the places to which the night-gaunts carry them.

Also, saying no to slumber will only anger the god Nodens, as he rules over dreamers and their lot. It is his duty and obligation to aid dreamers, even if the dreamer does not wish to sleep. Nodens will appear to the waker and forcefully carry them off to the Dreamlands. Whether that trip is done in the body or in the mind, Nodens cares not, for he is there to help others traverse the barriers between the Waking World and the Dreamlands. If you were too afraid to sleep, and to dream, the wrath of Nodens would be great, and you, as an undreamer, would be lost among the terrors of nightmares the next time sleep enfolds you. Saying no to slumber will be most unhealthy for the ones who are watched by Nodens, for in that watching comes the journey, whether it be wanted or not.

But I don't dream, so I think I am safe.

Nyarlathotep: The Original "Man in Black"

If Lovecraft had a personage in mind that would embody the quintessential characteristics of a charming serial killer, an amoral huckster, and a corrupt evangelist, Nyarlathotep would be that character. Nyarlathotep can appear as human, but he is a god, and thus can take any appearance he wishes. In fact, Nyarlathotep is truly a god of chaos; he has been known to take on several forms at will, and his plans are to wreak chaos and disorder at every turn. (He can even thwart his own intentions as times, as he is truly that chaotic!)

A god of the most evil ambitions, Nyarlathotep seeks to overthrow and thwart the intentions of all others. Could it be that Nyarlathotep is a kind of trickster deity? It would appear so, and if you are familiar with any trickster paradigm, this may be a way to understand his actions.

This god goes by many names, but it seems his favorite is *Nyarlathotep* or some variation thereof. (Yes, his name is a tongue twister!) Even though he is known as the messenger of the gods, Nyarlathotep's most common appellation is the Crawling Chaos. This moniker sums up what he does best. He works slowly, surely, but always for some sinister purpose. Nyarlathotep is not known as an impatient or imprudent god; in fact, he will only erupt in rage if many of his long-range plans collapse at once, and then his rage is short-lived. However fleeting his rage is, his memory is much longer, and this patience is most evident in those who seek to cross his path.

What is Nyarlathotep's purpose? To deceive, to entice, to enslave: all of these he wishes upon humanity. Why he does, no scholar can say, but because no one can find the reason for his enmity does not negate his enmity's existence.

No one knows what Nyarlathotep's natural form is, but most often when he appears he is a humanoid, dressed entirely in black clothes. As described by Lovecraft, Nyarlathotep favors the appearance of a human male, with deep Mediterranean features and skin so dark that it seems black.

(Black, here, is the actual color black, and does not describe the deep-colored skin tones of the peoples of the African continent. Also, Nyarlathotep's facial features do not denote someone with African heritage in their blood, but rather a classical Greek appearance as found in antique statuary from the Hellenistic period.)

Nyarlathotep is free to take on the appearance of any cultural group he deems appropriate to the occasion, but there will be a predominance of the ebony hue either to his skin color or, if he deigns to take on skin shades other than black, to his clothes. As I mentioned, his skin color is the actual color black, which is very unique, and can cause some to question his reality, especially when he is encountered in a solitary place when one is all alone.

When in human form, Nyarlathotep carries himself like royalty, and some occult students have commented that he originally hailed from ancient Egypt, where he was a pharaoh centuries ago. So is he a man who became a god? This is question to ponder, for it might explain some of his appearances and motivations. Being the Crawling Chaos, Nyarlathotep can take many forms, some of which are not even remotely human. But it is rumored that because he was a pharaoh centuries ago,

Nyarlathotep delighted in the humans' love of worshipping him as a living god (which he is), and so he has an odd, atavistic fondness for that form. As much as Nyarlathotep hates humanity, he seems to have some affection for people. Again, this might a relic of the days when he once walked the Earth and humanity counted him as one of their own.

Nyarlathotep delights in the technology of illusion, the devices that seem to border upon magic. In the days before the advent of electricity, Nyarlathotep did work magic to entice and entrance his human audience. But now, with this technology, Nyarlathotep is eager to utilize electricity, an invention that has helped humanity so much, in order to thwart people.

What is Nyarlathotep's mode of operation to dominate and thwart humanity? It takes two forms: mass appeal and personal allure.

First, let me discuss mass appeal. Nyarlathotep loves to preach to large throngs of people. Television and radio are part of his repertoire when it comes to seducing humans into becoming his followers. With the skill of an orator and the emotional charisma of a lover, Nyarlathotep gathers and sways large crowds to do his bidding. Often meeting in lecture halls or other venues that can support a vast number of people, Nyarlathotep, dressed in his customary black clothing, will lecture/entertain/sermonize/hypnotize the audience with whatever form of technology he is displaying, be it a simple ray of light shining from an unseen and unknown power source, or awesome displays of raw electrical power from towering cylinders. The blinding glare of the spotlights, the overpowering boom of his voice through a PA system: these Nyarlathotep will employ to appear larger than life, to act as a god among men.

The message that Nyarlathotep conveys is always changing: a new technology, a better way of life, a new religion, anything that gives the illusion of hope and future prosperity. With sadistic empathy, Nyarlathotep will delight in the despair that he senses from his followers when the new technology he touts causes radiation burns, the better way of life causes broken homes, and the new religion exterminates all those who differ in opinion.

Nyarlathotep unleashes the worst in humanity and all it can offer.

The second means is personal allure. This "man in black" will walk the Earth in the loneliest of places, there to meet and converse with unsuspecting humans. If Nyarlathotep so desires, that person may walk away unscathed, with little more than a slight memory loss as to the actual conversation. But if Nyarlathotep fancies that person, he will glibly talk that person into some sort of action that can result in death or dismemberment, usually not just involving the person in question. This conversation can be tempered by Nyarlathotep's charisma, which he chooses to amplify or downplay at will, the better to sway and sweet-talk his "prey."

By finding those sentiments and emotions that resound with his human partner, Nyarlathotep will exploit a niche in the psychic defense of the human and worm his way past fears and gut reactions, to overcome and corrupt even the staunchest of warriors and the most cynical of philosophers. Instead of cultivating true hope in a mass audience, Nyarlathotep will aim for any weakness to exploit, whether it be fear, love, vanity, or any other human emotion.

The Crawling Chaos also travels to the Dreamlands, there sowing the bitter seeds of discord and anarchy. In either world, the goal of Nyarlathotep is to show the humans an illusion, a hope they fervently wish to cling to, and to promise that illusion—so much so that the audience becomes his willing throng and thrall, and will gladly follow Nyarlathotep wherever he goes.

Wherever he goes. And sometimes Nyarlathotep will go in company with the horrors of the night and those who delight in human flesh. Nyarlathotep will feed these monsters with the flesh of his followers, who go gladly singing into the maws of their own doom.

Nyarlathotep is chaos personified, seemingly bringing order to disorder, but your actions, however noble and altruistic, are merely covert tools in his schemes to destroy humanity in the end. Trust your instincts and do not believe your eyes when dealing with anyone who may seem charismatic, who offers the wonders of technology as a means to elevate the human condition, or who extols the virtues of a new philosophy of love, for all these are but masks of the true horrors that lie on the other side.

Shantak-Birds:
Slippery Excursions, Inc.

The humans of the Dreamlands have access to common land-based mounts like we do on Earth: horses, mules, donkeys, and even elephants and zebras. But the dwellers in the Dreamlands also have at their command various flying steeds that have only existed in earthly fables and legends. One such example of these flying steeds is the common shantak-bird.

A shantak-bird is immense, and while it is comparable to the size of the fabled roc of Earth (or, more realistically, an elephant), the shantak-bird has scant resemblance to any earthly bird save in overall dispensation of appendages (a head and neck, a streamlined torso that boasts strong hind legs, a set of sweeping wings mounted at the animal's shoulders, and a snaking tail to act as an aerial rudder). Its bone structure is quite a bit sturdier than an avian frame, as there is some sort of magical element that enables such a large animal to stay aloft under its own muscles and will.

The head of this creature has no beak, but is very horse-like in shape and proportions (*hippocephalic* is the adjective Lovecraft used to encapsulate the animal's particular facial appearance). Covering the shantak-bird's body and wings are not downy feathers, but scales that are slippery to the touch due to their greasy coating. This property would appear at first to be an evolutionary feature that allows the creature to shed water or snow from its scales in order to enable it to keep flying in inclement weather. But that is not the case. The scaly "feathers" of these avian-like beasts are usually weather-stained, with either salt encrustations from the ocean air or even frost and ice from flying at higher altitudes. Shantak-birds do not generate heat from their bodies the way normal animals do, and this feature of their physiology seems to result in the build-up of cold-weather phenomena on their wings and bodies, in spite of the highly frictionless scales.

This slipperiness of their scaly feathers is phenomenal; the scales can be compared to an oiled glass surface in terms of their frictionless properties. But in spite of this, shantak-birds are highly regarded as an excellent mode of transportation.

Shantak-birds make their nests inside caves high atop mountain peaks, presumably as a defense against predation. While immense in size, shantak-birds have few natural enemies, and their most prevalent predators are humans themselves. The human inhabitants of the Dreamlands do not eat the birds for their coarse, unsavory flesh or slimy, colorless scales. Instead, the unhatched eggs are highly sought after and prized by culinary experts and epicures. Shantak-bird eggs are eaten as delicacies for feasts and special events, as the yolks and egg whites are savory and quite sensational to the palate. And, as expected, these eggs are enormous, and one egg, properly prepared, can feed up to five adult humans at one sitting. Tamed and domesticated shantak-birds will have their eggs harvested much like earthly chickens, save for one important difference. A human chicken farmer on Earth could gather eggs by himself only using a hand-held basket; a human shantak-bird farmer must gather eggs with a horse-drawn cart and help from a team of laborers.

Gathering shantak-bird eggs in the wild would be a nearly impossible task. Even if one came upon a nest, ideally at night when the shantak-birds normally sleep, the sheer size and weight of the cream-colored eggs make it difficult to carry away intact such a prize due to the remote and inaccessible locations of the rookeries.

As they are easily domesticated and tamed, shantak-birds can be compared to the horse in terms of intelligence and instincts. With proper care and firm but gentle training, shantak-birds can make excellent and faithful companions, in addition to their utilitarian function as steeds.

However, there do exist superior examples of these beasts, one of which has been called the King of the Shantaks due to its size and its propensity to behave as if it possessed a brain approaching the capacity of a human's. This bird is kept in a royal palace in the Dreamlands, in a sturdy cage that is always shielded from the light, as to make the king shantak-bird drowsy and pliable. (Woe be to anyone who allows daylight to shine upon this animal . . .)

Even though humans are the only real predator that can deplete the numbers of these large and ponderous animals, there is one species from which shantak-birds recoil in panic, even at the slightest hint of its presence. This species is the night-gaunt. Shantak-birds will flee wildly in terror and unbridled panic from anything related to night-gaunts, whether the sight of night-gaunts' lairs or the creatures themselves. What causes such an instinctive response in these birds from creatures that are puny in comparison to them is a mystery. However, if shantak-birds sufficiently outnumber any encountered night-gaunts—if, say, a flock of shantak-birds comes across a lone example of the inky-skinned "demon"—the shantaks will attack and attempt to drive off or kill their hated foe. Even a domesticated and well-behaved shantak-bird can be thrown into a frenzy at the smell of a night-gaunt's skin or the sight of a night-gaunt's cave lair.

It is common knowledge among the travelers of the Dreamlands' skies that using shantak-birds avoids any possibility of crossing night-gaunt territory. While it is a rare occurrence to espy a night-gaunt during daylight hours, it can happen, and such an event could throw an unwary or careless rider from his mount. And at night, when shantak-birds normally sleep, a night-gaunt incursion will cause these steeds to panic and soar into the air without regard for the well-being of their kin or human masters. A full-grown shantak-bird can do serious damage to a human with a brush of its wings and a misstep with its clawed talons. (Ranchers and horse trainers can attest to the tendency of horses to bolt and rear at the smell of open flames or the sight of a large predator; such is the same with shantak-birds with regard to the devilish night-gaunts. This natural instinct is difficult to quiet or eradicate in shantak-birds, so most riders are well aware of the effects of a night-gaunt presence.)

Given the slippery nature of their scales (and their enormous strength!), shantak-birds are difficult to control when upset. Even well-lashed and taut bridles and harnesses can slip and twist on their bodies in even the most mundane of aerial maneuvers, so extreme care is used when securing one's belongings and riding saddles on these animals.

Have you ever climbed onto a boulder or rocky slope after a rainstorm? The going can be treacherous. Now imagine that the boulder is alive and wriggling in response to your motions, and you have some idea about how hazardous it can be to ride a shantak-bird. Their feathers/scales would seem to offer reliable hand- and footholds, but the glassy and smooth surface that they do in fact have is not for the unwary or the novice handler.

Yet when treated with kindness and respect, a shantak-bird will be a docile and friendly companion for any traveler. The great distances they can cover in one day greatly outweigh the difficulties one may have in remaining stable on such a mount.

Shoggoths: Mr. Bubbles Cleans Down to the Bone

Have you ever seen a mass of soapsuds? Let me offer a solid example of what I mean here. A sink full of dirty dishes awaits you. They're not just any dishes, but your best china.

Bone china. The finest china available to you.

Today, your prized bone china is covered, nay, slathered with the remains of a Thanksgiving meal. Plenty of turkey meat and gravy covers each plate, smeared and almost a solid mass upon each plate.

The meal has been left on the plates for a long time. So long, in fact, that the plate and the meat have become one, as if each was meant to complement the other.

The plate is so filthy, so caked with protein leavings, that you cannot see its white surface. The turkey meat and gravy stand in the way of the lovely and oddly sparkling cleanliness of a new bone-china plate.

If only something could remove the pesky food and leave the bone china intact.

Aaah, there is such a cleanser: a bottle of liquid dish soap. You squirt it out onto the filthy plates. The mass of soap slides easily across the morass of meat solids. A dash of hot water and, voilà, the sink fills with clear, sudsy, cleansing bubbles. *How adorable*, you might think of the shimmering bubbles. "Harmless," you might say out loud, sinking your fingers into the buildup. "Wow," you might add, holding up the bone-china plate to the light, "that soap can really eat through all that grease!"

Now imagine the soapsuds as black. And bigger. Much bigger. Imagine each bubble as being yards across. This throng of bubbles, glistening black and oily, is now not just filling the sink, but the entire kitchen.

And this wall of black bubbles is alive, intelligent, searching.

Searching for more grease to clean.

Grease, which is bound to flesh and bone.

You.

Shoggoths, in their true state, resemble a mass of bubbles very much like those just-described soapsuds. The difference between this description and what you should imagine is not very much. A shoggoth's natural color is a tar-like glossy black, and its natural shape is very much akin to a mass of frothing soapsuds . . . only each "bubble" is yards across.

Their natural shape, that is.

The scientists of the elder things, who wanted a creature that could be specifically modified for each task it needed to complete, created shoggoths. Shoggoths by nature are animals manipulated and forced into monstrous shapes; thus, their natural shape is only achieved when at rest. When they are forced into obedience, shoggoths can alter their own bodies to create any needed appendage or required limb. For instance, if a shoggoth is required to clean out a chamber of accumulated filth, the shoggoth might elect to create thousands of licking tongues to scour the walls. And to dispose of the scraped-off filth, a rudimentary digestive system is developed to reprocess the dirt into something useful.

After all, the best way to clean is to recycle.

Created by possibly the greatest minds of our universe, shoggoths are the ultimate machines, servants, and guardians. When the elder things needed warriors to fight off the mi-goes or Cthulhu spawn, shoggoths filled the ranks, creating claws, fangs, or slashing tails as required. When the elder things needed something to harvest the underwater algae farms, shoggoths developed gills and webbed limbs to gather their watery produce. Whatever was needed, shoggoths adapted and filled that niche. When finished with their tasks, the shoggoths resumed their natural state, and went quietly back to their stables, which were also created by the elder things. Over the centuries, the elder things relied so much on their created servants that the elder things forgot simple tasks like farming, harvesting, and defending themselves from warring forces.

In its later days, the Roman Empire relied heavily on foreign subjects to defend its borders. Once these foreign soldiers realized they were completely in charge of the frontier's defense, they knew that nothing could stop them from going on the offensive and achieving their goal of gaining their freedom and overthrowing and sacking the cities of their masters.

So it was with the shoggoths.

But I digress. I want simply to describe these monsters. Omnivorous by nature, shoggoths are capable of forming mouths and appendages required to consume each particular meal they fancy. For grass and other vegetation, shoggoths have been reported to create whip-like appendages to shear and gather grass, which is then funneled into a spacious expanse of an intake orifice that resembles an enormous grin. To consume protein, shoggoths can develop razor-sharp teeth and claws to dissect and render the protein source into easily digestible amounts.

For any carnivore, the smaller the size of the protein meal, the more easily digestible it is. But the most readily available source of protein comes in large amounts. Stalking and killing pounds and pounds of flesh concentrated in one source is more energy-efficient than seeking out a large number of smaller protein sources. For this reason, lions choose to eat antelopes, not mice.

Maintaining the shoggoths' energy level was a concern of the creatures' creators, and elder things programmed the ability to withstand famine, drought, and extremes of temperature into their servants' construction, so that shoggoths could work in any clime or under any circumstance. Shoggoths could wait for years before feeding, and survive decades under water in the gloom of the ocean floor, content in their prearranged genetic engineering to remain obedient and docile. And shoggoths were keen to obey their masters, as their masters were kind enough to make them almost immortal.

A happy worker is one that toils forever, right?

To direct and order these beasts, the elder things developed telepathy. Using a mind link, an elder thing could direct a shoggoth in exactly what needed to be accomplished, right down to the type of body shape it should take. Such was the skill and power of the science of the elder things.

But as the centuries progressed, the elder things required more and more shapeshifting ability of their shoggoths, to complete more complicated and technological tasks. Instead of the elder things needing the shoggoths to, say, excavate a place for the nuclear-powered reactors built by the elder things, now the elder things needed the shoggoths to maintain and operate these reactors. And with these tasks, the shoggoths grew more intelligent.

Fiendishly intelligent.

Suffice it to say, the shoggoths broke free of their masters' yokes.

They became free to be whomever they wished to be. Or appeared to be.

Or simply, free to appear as their natural shape.

So whenever you find yourself on the shore of some placid lake in an idyllic pasture, or on the edge of a riverbank as it snakes through peaceful countryside, always make sure the bubbles you see quivering along the water's edge are actually soap bubbles, and not something more, something that would clean you . . . down to the bone.

Shub-Niggurath: Fecund Spawn of Unholy Horrors

Shub-Niggurath is an oft-prayed-to goddess and one of the more terrifying deities in the world of Lovecraft, due to her ability to inspire worship from mi-goes, evil sorcerers, witches, and other unwholesome beings. Since Lovecraft does not choose to horrify us with a complete picture of what Shub-Niggurath looks like (a dark, ropy monstrosity with large cloven-hoofed feet, of which there are many), it is up to us to figure out what she is from descriptions of her in the *Necronomicon* and the sorcerers who call upon her favors.

I have given Shub-Niggurath a female gender, as she is called the "Goat of a Thousand Young," implying that she is fecund and fertile. What she births and rears is not known, but considering that Lovecraft groups her into the same class as Cthulhu, Yog-Sothoth, and Nyarlathotep, it can be deduced that her creations work against the betterment and aims of humanity.

She is not on humanity's side, to put it mildly.

Shub-Niggurath has a cult-like following among humans, most notably among certain degenerate witch sects and sorcerers' covens. Presumably, Shub-Niggurath is called upon in some types of perverse fertility rites; when these rites are discovered by non-initiates, the police are immediately notified to check out the goings-on at such ceremonies, which implies that nothing legal can be determined at first glance. Such people who are captured and arrested by the police will confess to murder and obscene acts in order to appease their god, justifying the interlopers' call to the local sheriff department. Such obscene rituals are set forth in the *Necronomicon*, and the stoutest of hearts are averse even to reading the horrid rites that are set to curry Shub-Niggurath's favor.

Such rituals to call upon Shub-Niggurath are always set outdoors at certain times of the year, on rock altars built for such purposes. Whether these rituals use the energies of ley lines (magical concourses of natural energy) in their altar placement, or if Shub-Niggurath utilizes the harmonics of certain types of rocks in order for her to materialize in this dimension, is unknown. But the *Necronomicon*'s remark that the altar must be under open sky may mean that Shub-Niggurath needs the space in which to materialize. Shub-Niggurath will appear to those who know how to summon her and who approach her without fear.

Blood is a key ingredient to her summoning. Warm blood spilled from an intelligent creature usually works well for her followers. Fresh human blood seems to be the ticket; as for where the donated blood comes from, Shub-Niggurath is not that fussy.

Her cultish followers feel the same way. If they don't have a willing volunteer, they will take an unwilling one, even if it means one of their own. After all, Shub-Niggurath can make more of her kind . . .

Shub-Niggurath's form is difficult to ascertain due to the protean quality of the material body she chooses to use when conjured. According to some eyewitnesses, when Shub-Niggurath appears she can be towering in stature but uneasy to look upon, being mostly a black, ropy mass, as if immense tree trunks had fused and molded together. She walks upon multiple feet, in many directions at once, and her immense hooves can leave impressions in soft soil. The hoofed tracks, immense in size and seemingly placed in conflicting directions, are one of the well-known signals that a rite to Shub-Niggurath has been successfully performed.

Mi-goes worship Yog-Sothoth, but they prefer to worship Shub-Niggurath, and perform grotesque orgies upon their home world of Yuggoth to curry her favor, with the desired result of many offspring. It is not known if Shub-Niggurath actually copulates with the mi-goes, or is simply invoked as a fertility goddess. But when foul monsters worship fouler gods, I cannot imagine anything worse, so I will not even go into what might happen at such rituals. I will let your twisted imagination tackle that image.

One of the implied powers that Shub-Niggurath grants to her followers is the use or control of creatures she generates. Her cult will summon her, and Shub-Niggurath, if she looks favorably upon her followers, begets a fiend from her body so that the cult can use it for its evil purposes. This information comes from those arrested by the police, but I would not place much truck in their word, as torture can make a person say anything, especially to fearful public officials who choose to disregard the ominous sounds heard at altar sites late at night . . .

Animals instinctually fear the presence of Shub-Niggurath, and even those who worship her may provoke fear and

234

antipathy in animals. The power of Shub-Niggurath, which she instills in her followers with the obscene rites described in the *Necronomicon*, comes across as a palpable force or energy that dogs and cats can detect and to which they react. Whether this power is a residue of a successful contact, or a part of Shub-Niggurath that has been implanted into the worshipper, is a matter of conjecture. But in any event, normal animals will shun those who worship Shub-Niggurath and the places where she is worshipped or conjured.

So, if you are walking your dog in some desolate woods, and you come across large boulders, splashed with dark stains at the base and top, and your dog begins to howl and whimper, leave. Do not return to that spot, nor should you examine the cloven-hoof tracks in the mud surrounding the rocks, which look as though a herd of a cattle wandered around aimlessly on one or two legs. Nor should you ever admit to being at such a spot, especially if confronted by local people at whom your dog howls and barks like a possessed demon. Shub-Niggurath's cult just hates it when their sacred sites are intruded upon. They work *so* hard to bring her young to Earth that you should be thankful; so thankful, in fact, that you may be their guest of honor when they repurify the altar stone during the next new Moon . . .

Town of Arkham: Nice Place to Visit, but . . .

Although technically not a living creature, the town of Arkham takes on such a prominence in some of Lovecraft's stories that the community itself is a character, a character that holds dark secrets and salacious devils. So if it pleases you, I dub Arkham a monster in the Mythos.

In the stories of Lovecraft, the town of Arkham (better known simply as Arkham) is located in the state of Massachusetts, in Essex County. Located on both the north and south backs of the Miskatonic River (also an invention of Lovecraft's), Arkham was founded in the early seventeenth century by English settlers. These settlers had dealings with the disease-decimated natives of the region, who warned the invaders of strange monsters that dwelled in the hills surrounding the area. But still the immigrants came, sailing their ships up the Miskatonic to help turn the tiny hamlet into a thriving port town.

In the mid-1800s, the native population was gone, save for a few lone individuals who lived as recluses in the hills. The townspeople of Arkham ignored the former caretakers of the region, except when they sought answers as to why strange sounds came form the ground during certain times of the year, and why things, decomposing and unidentifiable, were found floating in the Miskatonic River from unknown places upriver . . .

Arkham boasts two institutions that have made it famous in the literary world, both again of Lovecraft's invention. The first is Miskatonic University, one of the few institutions of higher learning in the 1920s that offered a bachelor's degree in medieval metaphysics. Such courses lured the more esoteric students of arcane knowledge to this university, and also the attention of some of the more evil students and occultists. One of the prized collections in the university's library is an almost complete Latin edition of the *Necronomicon*, the only extant copy of this dreaded book in existence, which but a handful of the university professors there have read in its entirety and understood.

The second institution in Arkham is the Arkham Sanitarium, which has the dubious distinction of housing some of Miskatonic University's brightest minds (and some of its worst . . .). Many of Lovecraft's stories make reference to the sanitarium, which offers its services to those afflicted with ailments of both the mind and of the body. In fact, Arkham Sanitarium serves as an asylum for those who seek to restore mental clarity and calm, and for those whose nerves and cognitive functions are beyond hope. In the 1920s, going to a sanitarium to refresh and strengthen one's mental and physical states was a common medical cure. While one could be admitted involuntarily, the chances were that most people at a sanitarium were there voluntarily. People also retreated to sanitariums during epidemics, some of them forced there due to the severe nature of the contagion. This was an era before immunizations and vaccinations; influenza, diphtheria, and smallpox killed thousands across the land, and sanitariums offered aid and comfort to those afflicted.

However, in Lovecraft's Arkham, a trip to the sanitarium is *not* a good thing.

Many of the original structures built in Arkham during the seventeenth and early eighteenth centuries are still standing and inhabited. During the American War of Independence, smugglers in Arkham used tunnels, which connect the docks to warehouses, in order to confound the British authorities, but many of these tunnels were "rediscovered" ones that had also existed during Arkham's earlier history. Who or what built the tunnels is not clear, but what is clear is that few venture into those tunnels alone.

A rite of passage among certain fraternities at Miskatonic University involves a pledge traveling into one of these smugglers' tunnels at night and etching his name on a wall reserved for such a purpose. Most pledges who do so never speak of the experience—not because of the vow of secrecy that is part of such initiations, but out of fear of ridicule if they were to discuss what they spied in those damp, decaying tunnels: things that looked human but weren't . . .

Due to its numerous donors and benefactors (many of whom acquired their wealth from fishing or overseas trade), the university in Arkham has sponsored expeditions to locations around the globe, expeditions in search of ancient civilizations or to explore unknown locations.

In the 1920s the world still had places that knew not the tread of European feet, or even of any humans, and Miskatonic University prided itself on being able to finance and equip such expeditions to remote regions of the globe. Miskatonic University has sent its students and faculty to gather data from many continents, including Africa, Antarctica, and Australia, as well as hosting archaeological digs in various locations in the United States. These expeditions yield a great wealth of information about past societies and civilizations, some of which should never have been brought to the attention of historians . . .

Lovecraft set up the town of Arkham around the structure of the real city of Salem, Massachusetts, and completed the town's history with real and imagined witchcraft trials, the likes of which have reverberated down throughout the centuries. The tourism slogan of Arkham could be "What has happened in the past in Arkham does not tend to stay in Arkham's past."

Like so much else from Arkham's history, many monsters tend to accumulate in this town. Arkham is a nice place to visit during the daytime, but I never would want to live there. I don't need the *Necronomicon* to tell me that!

241

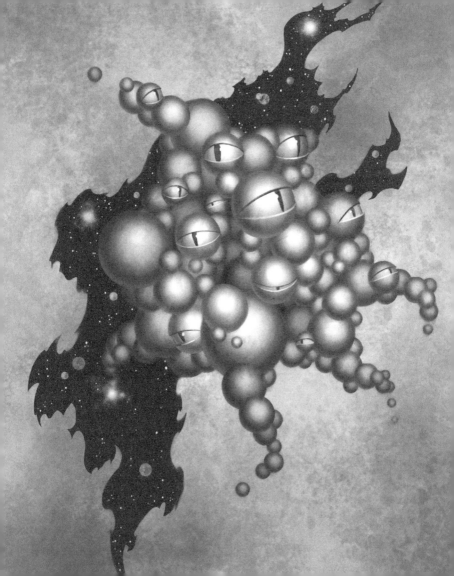

Yog-Sothoth:
An Open Doorway to . . . ?

None of the deities Lovecraft crafted are clearly defined in terms of what their roles and relatives are. Lovecraft used a variety of terms (the *Old Ones*, the *Elder Gods*, the *Great Old Ones*) to label groups of gods, but with little regard as to defining what he meant, even using contradictory material in his stories. Such is one of the puzzles of the Cthulhu Mythos.

Much has been written about who these Elder Gods are. But what has been constant in the discussion is the role of Yog-Sothoth as a doorway to these Old Ones. Yog-Sothoth's name was apparently one of Lovecraft's favorites, as he named his body of the Mythos *Yog-Sothothery*, although the moniker *Cthulhu Mythos* won out. I am glad, for *Yog-Sothothery* is such a tongue twister, and an open invitation to accidentally spit on whomever you are talking to.

I imagine Yog-Sothoth is upset at this. The naming of the Mythos, that is, not the social awkwardness of saying *Yog-Sothothery* in polite company.

In the various occult texts and lore found in the stories of Lovecraft, Yog-Sothoth is a doorway, perhaps the doorkeeper himself, one that allows (or disallows) the passage of deities, monsters, and travelers from one realm to another. This much is known for certain about Yog-Sothoth. He is also known as the Doorway, or the Key to the Gate. Perhaps he is known by other names as well, but this is not certain.

What is less known is what his actual appearance is, as few, if any, have seen him directly. I use the masculine pronoun to describe Yog-Sothoth simply because Lovecraft did not mention any specifically female deities, so don't let the word *he* make you think that Yog-Sothoth is by any means male. He may have been female, or neither, or both, or something else. One eyewitness described the god as a mass of cosmic bubbles, folding and bending back upon himself. Perhaps what this eyewitness saw were the doorways themselves, doorways to other realms or planes of existence.

Perhaps Yog-Sothoth is a shoggoth, a cosmically monstrous shoggoth, one that is set to devour the entire universe, doorway by doorway.

No, I think not. Too preposterous.

Way too preposterous, now that I reflect on it.

Yog-Sothoth is invoked by sorcerers who wish to call and control otherworldly beings, much like medieval magicians who cast a pentagram on the floor to trap and contain demons form the netherworlds. Like these medieval magicians, sorcerers in the Lovecraft stories obtain their lore from forbidden books of occult knowledge, the most famous of these being the *Necronomicon*. In this book are laid out the rituals and requirements to obtain Yog-Sothoth's aid in opening the doorways to other dimensions.

One of the devices mentioned in the *Necronomicon* is the Elder Sign, a sigil talisman that can compel or repel beings form the other side. When properly constructed, the Elder Sign acts much like a cross does to the legendary vampire. The Elder Sign is used in Lovecraft's stories to bind or block doorways from being utilized by the Old Ones or Elder Gods. The Elder Sign is used, to make a crude metaphor, as a stoplight for traffic from the outer worlds. In the *Necronomicon*, spells are laid out on how to force Yog-Sothoth to open and close the correct doorway.

Most magical tomes (and even fantasy and the swords-and-sorcery genre of books) have rituals to open doorways to alien and exotic locales, the likes of which are home to strange and wondrous monsters. But why would there be so many texts that tell of doorways to these varying worlds? Perhaps it is the widespread goal of humans to be able to travel. Perhaps it is the goal of the Elder Gods to travel. Perhaps it is both. But travel they wish, and travel they do. And Yog-Sothoth is a doorman, opening and closing doors for those who wish to leave or enter.

Like a doorman, Yog-Sothoth is selective about whom he heeds. Most ceremonies to invoke or call Yog-Sothoth involve a sacrifice on the part of the sorcerer.

A human sacrifice.

A live human sacrifice.

When a ritual is done properly, and Yog-Sothoth does grant the sorcerer access, the opened doorway may remain opened. It is not up to Yog-Sothoth to determine when and for how long a door will stay active. Indeed, negligent sorcerers have overlooked this important fact, and after they have obtained what they required from Yog-Sothoth, they forget that others may come through the door. After all, a door that opens allows any to pass through from either side of the threshold. It is usually the Elder Sign, appropriately placed at the ritual site, which closes or blocks a doorway from being used again. (Incidentally, the Elder Sign is commonly depicted as a cursive pentagram. Lovecraft, however, thought of the Elder Sign as a line drawing, a straight stick boasting five projections, much like a tree branch.) Moving the invoked Elder Sign will usually allow Yog-Sothoth entrance to that point previously blocked—much to the mover's chagrin, I might add.

Invoking Yog-Sothoth is a two-way street. Sometimes, the "others" on the other side of the doorway simply want a human meal. Home delivery, if you will. A "pizza" delivered, with all the meat that one craves, for a supper, but the box that holds the meal is not cardboard, but skin.

Carry-out, in a fleshy package.

And Yog-Sothoth is merely the pizza delivery boy. What he is delivering depends on who called first. When you think you have successfully conjured Yog-Sothoth to do your bidding, in fact it may actually be someone on the other side who successfully conjured Yog-Sothoth to set up a gateway to a warm, waiting meal!

Zoogs: Cute, Cuddly, but . . .

Zoogs are small but highly intelligent animals who inhabit the Dreamlands, growing in adulthood to a size comparable to that of terrestrial rabbits. Zoogs have been known to cross into the Waking World on numerous occasions, but only at those geographic locations on our Earth where the boundaries between the realms are thin and easily traversed by those skilled in dreaming. Thus, it is rare to spot a zoog on Earth, save for at those secret or unknown gates that link our world to that of the zoogs, and even then the zoogs are adept at hiding in shadows or remaining unseen, for these darling animals are very shy and reclusive at first.

To human perceptions, zoogs are rather adorable in appearance, with large eyes that most people find irresistible.

A typical zoog is brown in color, with a glossy hide akin to a hairless cat, with four legs. Each leg ends in dexterous claws, which enable the zoogs to climb trees and fashion crude instruments such as drills, shovels, and containers of hollowed-out wood or woven leaves. Arboreal by choice, zoogs can also burrow underground to form warrens for their communities of family units.

Living in tree trunks (zoogs do not build nests like squirrels, but will chew or claw their way into dead or easily removed wood, using primitive hand tools if need be) and highly intelligent (their small size is very deceptive; when they hunt, zoogs are equal, if not superior, in cunning and tactics to most pack animals of Earth), zoogs have a primitive culture, social cohesion, and language. The latter can be learned with much patience and offerings of food treats to a zoog. Zoogs love fungi, the kind that grows on trees native to the Dreamlands. They brew/ferment a delicious mead from the sap of these trees in their woods, and this mead can be flavored with the aforementioned fungi for a sweet or bitter taste, depending on the brewer's recipe.

But the zoogs have a fondness for meat, especially any meat carried by a dreamer from the Waking World or by humans who already live in the Dreamlands.

When I say *meat carried*, I don't mean meat lugged in backpacks or pouches, but on the very bones of the travelers themselves.

Zoogs are omnivorous, but being carnivorous is a taste-inspired lifestyle choice for them.

Did I mention they are cute? Even though their mouths are pinkish and they have a row of drooping, smallish tentacles on their upper lips (think of the earthly star-nosed mole but with a mustache of feelers), it is their eyes that give the illusion of peaceful intentions. (If you have ever seen a picture of a lemur, you know its wide and staring ocular organs can be quite lovely.) Zoogs behave quite shyly when approached for the first time. It is not that they are naturally skittish; they just are not sure what to make of strangers. Zoogs are not hunted by humans, and their natural predators are any that can grab zoogs from their trees or fit into their burrows—animals such as hawks or foxes.

With a limited vocabulary in their natural language, zoogs are expressive in face and eyes. If you want to know what a zoog is thinking, look into its eyes. Chances are, those eye-balls gazing back at you are full of cheer and good nature.

But when those same eyes are upon you and the zoog's tongue flicks in and out of its tentacle-mustachioed mouth, you had better be alert and willing to run. While most zoogs are "civilized" and curious, but wary of strangers, there are zoogs who do not conform to the "nice" behaviors of society. These zoogs tend to view strangers as something new to try, something different to fill their bellies. And these zoogs are not disinclined to urge others of their own kind to a frenzied bloodlust in order to overcome a larger "prey."

Zoogs: cute and cuddly, with the appetite of a killer.

When attacking, zoogs will swarm over their prey. One zoog is no match for a full-grown human, but thirty or so of these furry fiends are. Once the zoogs have selected a target, in particular the meaty appendages of a Waking World trav-eler, zoogs will stalk their prey at leisure, making their attack in one coordinated maneuver. Targets are selected by each zoog as the hunt commences. Some zoogs attack the throat and face, others the groin or stomach, others the tendons of the legs or the ankles. Zoogs will tear and feast even as their prey flees, much like a piranha pack attacking a cow in water.

If coerced, zoogs will negotiate for peace from superior foes. Zoogs may be bloodthirsty at times, but they are "quick on the uptake" if surrounded or if the attack is going badly for them. The instinct for survival is strong in this species, and they will find it better to live in peace in the shadow of an enemy than to be eradicated utterly. Even then, zoogs will be plotting to turn the tables, although the elders of the zoog communities will attempt to ensure that other zoogs honor the terms of any contract negotiated.

A traveler to the Dreamlands might be tempted to take one of these furry creatures home as a pet, or even use one as a guide through the zoog woods, but I would advise against this. As adorable as these little fellows might appear, I would not want to let my guard down with one, especially if I were sleepy and wanting to go to bed.

You don't know if you might wake up to the sounds of your own throat being chewed out by your "cuddly" pet.

Fin

This concludes my guided tour of the monsters of the Mythos, the collection of creatures coiled to pounce and prey upon humanity. I hope you enjoyed yourself.

In the next section I offer a suggested reading list of the prose writings of Lovecraft that I have particularly enjoyed and feel would be of a benefit to you as a newcomer to the world of H. P. Lovecraft.

I do apologize if I concerned you at all with my tone at any time during this reading. I am quite capable of rational thought and expression when need be, but I do get carried away sometimes.

Sometimes the night-gaunts carry me.

Other times it can be a gug. And I will even let myself be carried away by Cthulhu himself.

But whatever carries me over into the realm of the unholy, the unearthly, the unsavory, I show the creatures, in their leering faces, my diploma from Miskatonic University, and then wave my certificate that I am certifiably not insane, a certificate signed by myself, in the presence of myself.

In crayon.

On a napkin.

Onward, faithful steed! Let us explore further!

Wheeee!!!

A Selected H. P. Lovecraft Bibliography
(in no particular order)

I have chosen the following tales, all of which I recommend highly, from the list of Lovecraft's works. If you are curious and wish to read the stories as Lovecraft himself laid them out, seek out these stories and enjoy them. Most good bookstores will carry them, but since Lovecraft wrote primarily short stories, you will need to examine the table of contents of any Lovecraft anthology to see what tales are collected in that particular edition. I would recommend any collection that contains words such as *The Best of Lovecraft* in its title, as some anthologies will print Lovecraft's earlier works. While not as polished as their later counterparts, you still might want to read these early tales for the simple act of expanding your knowledge about the Mythos.

As with enjoying any horror tales, I suggest you read these stories in a setting you might deem conducive. With the advent of books on electronic screens, it is now possible to read in the dark without the aid of any external lighting. I dare you to read these tales while sitting alone in totally darkened room, save for the translucent rays of the computer screen . . .

1. "The Call of Cthulhu." This short story is the basis for understanding the god Cthulhu and his dark designs upon the Earth. A masterful tale, the story follows one man's odyssey to piece together the cult of Cthulhu. This story is a good introduction to the horror writing style of Lovecraft, and is well regarded by critics as one of Lovecraft's most masterful tales.

2. "The Statement of Randolph Carter." Here's a fine example to introduce you to Lovecraft's prolific word use in such a small tale. Don't let this story escape your Lovecraft research! In a typical Lovecraftian structure, this story is a first-person narration of the horrors that

the main character has experienced while exploring forbidden occult territories.

3. "The Outsider." Grab a dictionary and seat yourself in a dreary room. This story combines the horror and "weird" elements of Lovecraft's style, in order to create an allegory of personal alienness and acceptance.

4. "Pickman's Model." A very scary short story, one that easily transcends the era in which it was written. Not for the squeamish (though mild compared to today's graphic horror descriptions), this tale incorporates delicious dark humor to hammer home the horror.

5. *The Shadow Over Innsmouth*. A longer tale, a novella actually, this work of horror is about one man's fight with an overwhelmingly superior foe, the deep ones. Not for the paranoid or those afraid of the water.

6. "The Cats of Ulthar." A short piece of prose writing, this work is a good introduction to the "weird fantasy" style of Lovecraft, and this tale is referenced many times in his *Dream-Quest of Unknown Kadath*-themed stories (see the next entry). Start here if you want the

weird fantasy feel (or to understand how cats are man's best friend!).

7. "The Silver Key." This is considered the finest work of Lovecraft's weird fantasy tales. A gold mine of information about the monsters and machinations of the Cthulhu Mythos, this tale tells of the travels of a human dreamer into the Dreamlands. If you enjoy the writing style of the first few paragraphs, you have been duly warned that this book will fire your imagination and dreaming. Many consider this tale the bulwark of the *Dream-Quest* stories.

8. *At the Mountains of Madness.* A novella, this classic horror story of an expedition sent out to explore Antarctica is gripping in its twists and turns. Written in a calm, detached, scientific voice, this book has been the inspiration for two famous science-fiction movies.

9. "The Dunwich Horror." A monster is set loose upon the New England landscape, and it is up to a small band of scholars and occultists to stop the beast. This tale lays out details of Lovecraft's Miskatonic University, and

expands the details of the fabled *Necronomicon*. Another example of Lovecraft's finer horror outings.

10. "The Rats in the Walls." Macabre horror—pure, unbridled, chilling horror. Not for the faint of heart or the weak of stomach. After reading this story, you'll think twice about investigating the weird sounds your house makes . . .

11. "The Lurking Fear." If this story doesn't scare the beejeebers out of you, I suggest you move on to another horror writer. If this warning does not dissuade you, don't say you haven't been warned!

12. "Supernatural Horror in Literature." This essay epitomizes Lovecraft's scholarship as it related to his craft of horror stories. In it, Lovecraft gives a rationale for why people read and write horror stories, as well as for their place in culture (Western culture, that is). Also included is a very thorough review of the Western literary types who contributed to the shape of horror writing as it existed in the late 1920s and early 1930s. I recommend this book to anyone who wants a firm background in understanding Lovecraft's rationale for

his stories, as well as for those who want to understand how Lovecraft perceived his place in the long tradition of Western literature. For an extra bonus, secure a copy of an annotated version, for in this essay Lovecraft refers to many other authors and works, some of which may now be obscure to the reader.

To Write to the Author

If you wish to contact the author or would like more information about this book, please write to the author in care of Llewellyn Worldwide and we will forward your request. Both the author and publisher appreciate hearing from you and learning of your enjoyment of this book and how it has helped you. Llewellyn Worldwide cannot guarantee that every letter written to the author can be answered, but all will be forwarded. Please write to:

T. Allan Bilstad
c/o Llewellyn Worldwide
2143 Wooddale Drive, Dept. 978-0-7387-1379-3
Woodbury, MN 55125-2989, U.S.A.

Please enclose a self-addressed stamped envelope for reply, or $1.00 to cover costs. If outside the U.S.A., enclose an international postal reply coupon.

Free Catalog

Get the latest information on
our body, mind, and spirit products!
To receive a **free** copy of Llewellyn's consumer
catalog, *New Worlds of Mind & Spirit,* simply call
1-877-NEW-WRLD or visit our website at
www.llewellyn.com and click on *New Worlds.*

LLEWELLYN ORDERING INFORMATION

Order Online:
Visit our website at www.llewellyn.com, select your books, and order them on
our secure server.

Order by Phone:
- Call toll-free within the U.S. at 1-877-NEW-WRLD
  (1-877-639-9753). Call toll-free within Canada at
  1-866-NEW-WRLD (1-866-639-9753)
- We accept VISA, MasterCard, and American Express

Order by Mail:
Send the full price of your order (MN residents add 6.875% sales tax) in
U.S. funds, plus postage & handling to:

> **Llewellyn Worldwide**
> **2143 Wooddale Drive, Dept. 978-0-7387-1379-3**
> **Woodbury, MN 55125-2989**

Postage & Handling:

Standard (U.S., Mexico & Canada). If your order is:
$24.99 and under, add $4.00
$25.00 and over, FREE STANDARD SHIPPING

AK, HI, PR: $16.00 for one book plus $2.00 for
each additional book.

International Orders (airmail only):
$16.00 for one book plus $3.00 for each additional book

Orders are processed within 2 business days.
Please allow for normal shipping time. Postage and handling rates subject to change.

Necronomicon

DONALD TYSON

The first *Necronomicon* created in the true spirit of H. P. Lovecraft!
Anyone familiar with Lovecraft's work knows of the *Necronomicon*,
the black-magic grimoire he invented as a literary prop in his classic
horror stories. There have been several attempts at creating this text,
yet none stand up to Lovecraft's own descriptions . . . until now.

This grimoire traces the wanderings of Abdul Alhazred, a nec-
romancer of Yemen, in his search for arcane wisdom and magic.
Alhazred's magical adventures lead him to encounter a variety of
strange creatures and to accrue necromantic secrets.

978-0-7387-0627-6, 288 pages $17.95

Alhazred
Author of the Necronomicon

DONALD TYSON

H. P. Lovecraft's compelling character Abdul Alhazred is brought to life in this epic tale detailing the mad sorcerer's tragic history and magical adventures. Here, Alhazred tells his own life story, beginning as a poor, handsome boy in Yemen who attracts the attention of the king. Young Abdul lives a luxurious life at the palace, studying necromancy and magic and falling in love with the king's daughter. Later, he joins a tribe of ghouls, learning forbidden secrets from a stranger called Nyarlathotep.

And thus begins his downward spiral into wickedness . . .

978-0-7387-0892-8, 672 pages $29.95

Grimoire of the Necronomicon

DONALD TYSON

On the heels of his widely successful *Necronomicon*, *Alhazred*, and *Necronomicon Tarot*, Donald Tyson now unveils a true grimoire of ritual magic inspired by the Cthulhu Mythos. The *Grimoire of the Necronomicon* is a practical system of ritual magic based on Lovecraft's mythology of the alien gods known as the Old Ones.

Tyson expands upon their mythology and reintroduces these "monsters" in a new, magical context—explaining their true purpose for our planet. Daily rituals provide an excellent system of esoteric training for individual practitioners. This grimoire also provides structure for an esoteric society—the Order of the Old Ones—devoted to the group practice of this unique system of magic.

978-0-7387-1338-0, 216 pages $18.95

To order, call 1-877-NEW-WRLD
Prices subject to change without notice
Order at Llewellyn.com 24 hours a day, 7 days a week!

The Magick Bookshop
Stories of the Occult
KALA TROBE

In this occult novel, myth and magick come to life in a small English bookshop. The books in Malynowsky's Bookshop both lure and intimidate, and the clientele come to browse knowing that their needs will be met and their privacy respected.

This collection of six short stories takes you inside this little world of mystery, real magick, and moral lessons. Meet Paul Magwitch, possessed by the spirit of a young girl who compels him to buy expensive things he does not want; the Witch in the City, who ekes out a living reading Tarot for strangers; and Eurydice, a shop employee who becomes the victim of a customer's magickal attack.

978-0-7387-0515-6, 240 pages $15.95

Magick in the West End

Stories of the Occult

KALA TROBE

Step inside Malynowsky's Central, a bookstore teeming with tomes on magick and esoteric lore. Kala, who brought us inside a fascinating otherworld in *The Magick Bookshop*, continues her urban forays into Witchcraft and the occult at this not-so-ordinary bookshop in modern-day London. These seven vivid tales are filled with metaphysical happenings and unforgettable characters—including the wise shop owner, who helps Kala break free from an unhealthy downward spiral that threatens everything dear to her.

978-0-7387-0779-2, 192 pages $14.95

The Pagan Anthology of Short Fiction

13 Prize Winning Tales

PRESENTED BY LLEWELLYN AND *PANGAIA* MAGAZINE

This fresh medley of never-before-published Pagan fiction is the result of a contest launched by Llewellyn and *PanGaia* magazine. A jury headed by popular author Diana Paxson pored over hundreds of entries and selected thirteen of the very best.

From historic to contemporary fiction, fantasy to erotica, romance to science fiction, these compelling tales span literary styles and a variety of Pagan traditions.

Redemption, self-acceptance, justice, love, and death are all explored in this remarkable anthology.

978-0-7387-1269-7, 240 pages $18.95